JAMAICAN CREOLE
GRAMMAR

I'HESHIA HANDY

JAMAICAN
CREOLE
GRAMMAR

ISBN: 979-8-9857370-1-1

Acknowledgements

The author would like to thank family and friends for their support and encouragement of the endeavor to undertake this project. Special thanks to: Shantana Dyer, Camille Green-Wright, Nerissa Noad, Elva Rose, Oshane Sinclair, Byanka White, and Alexia Wright.

Contents

Introduction

When West African people were brought by the British to the West Indies to work as slaves, they spoke many different languages and dialects. Through forced assimilation, people were required to interact with other people who spoke different languages than themselves. This created a need for a common language.

A language emerged from the difficult circumstances of slavery, and this language was Jamaican Creole. It can be thought of as a hybrid language that combines English and West African languages. Words such as *pikni* or *pikini* and *nyam* are often referenced by Jamaicans to be of West African origin. That said, Jamaican Creole has a lot of English or English-sounding words.

While English is the official language of Jamaica, people speak Jamaican Creole with family and friends. In fact, some people speak Jamaican Creole as their first language. Additionally, the language is spoken on a continuum, ranging from what many Jamaicans would regard as 'raw patois' to almost English. In schools and other formal settings, however, people speak standard English. This book compares the grammatical structures of Jamaican Creole and English to help you develop a better understanding of the differences between the two languages.

Jamaican Creole is not a formal language, so there might be a variety of spellings for a particular word when it is written by different people. This book uses the simplest spelling for each syllable of a word to imitate the spoken word as best as possible. The words most commonly used in everyday conversation are used in the examples and exercises included.

In this book are lessons that will help you to compare the grammatical structures of Jamaican Creole and English. It is suggested that you use the book *Jamaican Creole Tenses* along with this book to improve your understanding of Jamaican Creole.

Abbreviations Used in this Book

adj.	adjective
adv.	adverb
contr.	contraction
E.	English
JC.	Jamaican Creole
lit.	literally
n.	noun
n/a	not applicable
prep.	preposition
sing.	singular
v.	verb
v. phrase	verb phrase

Contractions Used in Jamaican Creole

Certain contractions that are used in English are not used in Jamaican Creole. The following list includes contractions that are used in Jamaican Creole along with their uncontracted meaning and English meaning.

> A **contraction** is a shortened version of a word or the combination of two or more words to form a single word.

Jamaican Creole Contractions	Uncontracted Meaning	English Meaning
aggo	a goh	is going
anno	a noh	is not
dideh	deh deh; bi deh	am/is/are there; be there
didehsoh	deh dehsoh	is there; are there
dwiit	duh ih/duh it	do it
fihit	fi it	for it; its
fiit	fi it	for it; its
gaa	goh a	go to
giim	gi him/gi im	give him
gimmi	gi mi	give me; give it to me

Jamaican Creole Contractions	Uncontracted Meaning	English Meaning
gwaan	goh aan	go on
haffi	ha fi	have to
indeh	inna deh	in there
inna'ih	inna di	in the
leggo	let goh	let go
miit	mi ih/mi it	me it (e.g., *Gi miit* (E. *Give me it*))
neev'n	not iiv'n/noh iiv'n	not even; does not even;
		do not even; did not even;
		has not even; have not even
neev'n did	not iiv'n did/noh iiv'n did	did not even; had not even
niiv'n	not iiv'n/noh iiv'n	not even; does not even;
		do not even; did not even;
		has not even; have not even
niiv'n did	not iiv'n did/noh iiv'n did	did not even; had not even
noffi	noh fi	ought not to; should not
pudong	put dong	put down
siim	si him/si im	see him
siit	si ih/si it	see it
sisso	seh soh	say so
waa	wa a	what is
wii	wi wi	we will
y'a	yuh a	you are

Pronunciation of Jamaican Creole Words

A guide to the pronunciation of vowels, consonants, and diphthongs follows with an example of a word imitating the sound. Refer to them as often as necessary.

Vowels

a- sharp *a*, as in *wrap*

e- sharp *e*, as in *bet*

i- sharp *i*, as in *zip*

o- sharp *o*, as in *dove*

u- sharp *u*, as in *put*

û- pronounced like the *i* in *first* and the *u* in *murmur*

Consonants

C is pronounced like English *k*, except before *h*.

Ch is pronounced like the ch in *chicken*.

G is pronounced like the *g* in *get* before and after vowels. After consonants, it has a softer sound like the *g* in *hang*.

S is pronounced like the *s* in *sew*.

Consonant combinations are generally used as they are in English, e.g., *ng, rt, nk, nt*, etc. The exception is *ph* where *p* and *h* have distinct sounds when used in Jamaican Creole. An example of this is *japhan* (a type of informal savings program where people pool their money together and take turns getting lump sum payments). It comes from the English words *drop* and *hand*.

Diphthongs

See the pronunciation of diphthongs below.

> A **diphthong** is a combination of two vowels that is pronounced as a single syllable. The letter *y* is sometimes used in diphthongs, although it is not generally considered a vowel.

aa- pronounced like the long *a* sound in *bath*

ai- pronounced like *ai* in *Taiwan*

au- pronounced like *au* in *augment*

ay- pronounced like *ay* in *aye*

ee- pronounced like *a* in *spray*

ia- pronounced like the *ia* in *Gambia*

ii- pronounced like the *ee* in *queen*

oo- pronounced like the long *o* sound in *float*

ou- pronounced like *ou* in *out*

ua- pronounced like *ua* in *Guatemala*

uo- pronounced *uh-wo*

uu- pronounced like the *oo* sound in *afternoon*

ya- pronounced like the *ya* in *yap*

yaa- pronounced like the *ya* in *kumbaya*

ye- pronounced like the *ye* is *yes*

yu- pronounced like *ew* sound in *nephew* or like *you* in *youth*

Using Superscripts to Label Jamaican Creole and English Words

In order to make it easier to read Jamaican Creole sentences, it is suggested that you place *E* superscript above the first letter of English words if the sentence has more Jamaican Creole words, and place *J* superscript above the first letter of Jamaican Creole words if the sentence has more English words. It is also less time-consuming to label the least amount of words, and this will make it easier to determine how to pronounce the words in the sentence. For example:

Dem aggo si wa mi a ^{E}talk bout.

In the following sentence, there are more English words, so we label the Jamaican Creole words.

^{J}Mi planning to ^{J}goh Nigeria.

Equal Numbers of Jamaican Creole and English Words

If a sentence has an equal number of Jamaican Creole and English words, label only the words in the language of the first word. For example:

^{J}Shi travel often ^{J}goh ^{J}a Kingston.
^{E}Paul a mi fren ^{E}from ^{E}school.

When a sentence has only Jamaican Creole or English words, the words do not need to be labeled with *J* or *E*. For example:

Mi iht lyet inna di iivlin.

John moving to St. Mary.

In the first example, all the words are in Jamaican Creole. In the second example, all words are in English.

Using Subscripts to Label Jamaican Creole and English Words

There are certain words that resemble the English words that they came from, and only the last few letters of the words are changed. Some words with the last few letters changed include *further, burger, river*, and *sulfur*. It is suggested that you write *J* subscript before these last few letters to let the reader know that they should pronounce those letters using the Jamaican Creole alphabet. For example, *further* would become *fur_Jda*, *burger* would become *burg_Ja*, *river* would become *riv_Ja*, and *sulfur* would become *sulf_Ja*. Also, one could use the Jamaican alphabet to spell the entire word (*fûrda*, *bûrga*, *riva*, and *solfa*), though this can sometimes make it more difficult to determine what English words they came from.

For compound words with the first word in Jamaican Creole and the second word in English, it is suggested that you label the English portion of the word with *E* subscript beginning with the first letter. For example, the compound word *handbag* is *han_Ebag* in Jamaican Creole. If the first word were labeled *E*, then you might mistakenly pronounce the entire word using the English alphabet. When the first word is in English and the second word is in Jamaican Creole, the Jamaican Creole word is labeled with *J* subscript. An example of this is *news_Jpyepa*.

Consonant Sounds
The 'th' Sound

The 'th' sound is absent in Jamaican Creole and is replaced by the 't' sound in most cases. Some examples are:

tyeta	*theatre*
tûrmos	*thermos*
tik	*thick*
tonda	*thunder*

In some cases (primarily pronouns and adverbs), the 'd' sound is used to replace the 'th' sound at the beginning of certain words. Some examples are:

dyer *there*	den *then*	duoz *those*
dis *this*	dat *that*	dem *them*
diiz *these*	dan *than*	di *the*

demself *themselves*   deeh *they*

When 'th' occurs between two vowels, the 'd' sound is frequently used to replace it. Some examples are:

wedda	*weather*
faada	*father*
bredda	*brother*

When 'th' occurs at the end of a word, it is usually replaced by 't'. Some examples are:

baat	*bath*
naat	*north*
paat	*path*

Not all words follow the previous rule. *Wid* (E. *with*) is one such word that does not follow this rule.

The 'R' Sound

The letter 'r' is usually only pronounced when it occurs at the beginning or at the end of a word. When the letter occurs elsewhere in a word, the letter is usually omitted. Some examples are:

kyaar	*car*
kyaat	*cart*
rispek	*respect*
wol	*world*

An exception to this rule is the Jamaican Creole word *wûrl*. It is pronounced like E. *world* without the *d*.

In most cases, a long 'a' sound (pronounced like 'a' in path) is used to replace 'ar' and 'or' when they occur between two consonants. Some examples are:

faak	*fork*
kyaapet	*carpet*
laad	*lord*
maak	*mark*
paak	*park*
shaap	*sharp*

When 'er', 'or', 'ar', 'ur', and 'ure' occur at the end of a word, they are frequently replaced by a sharp 'a'. Some examples are:

directa	*director*
filta	*filter*
pikcha	*picture*
pilla	*pillar*
solfa	*sulfur*
waata	*water*

When 'd' and 'r' occur together, the combination is often pronounced like 'j'. Some examples are:

jaah	*draw*
jaiva	*driver*
jap	*drop*

When Consonants Are Used Together

When two consonants are used together within or at the end of a word, Jamaicans usually omit one of these letters (or replace both with another letter in a small number of cases). Some examples are:

aat	*art*
tugedda	*together*
wid	*with*
wol	*world*

'D' is frequently omitted when it occurs after 'n' or 'l' at the end of a word. Some examples are:

an	*and*
ben	*bend*
buol	*bold*
dimaan	*demand*
guol	*gold*
kuol	*cold*

In cases where 's' occurs before 'm' in an English word, the vowel 'u' is frequently inserted between the two letters in Jamaican Creole. An 'i' is inserted in some words. Examples are:

simell	*smell*
sumaal	*small*
sumuok	*smoke*

When 's' occurs before 'n', an 'i' is frequently inserted between them. Examples are:

siniiz	*sneeze*
sinuo	*snow*
sinyek	*snake*

'S' is occasionally omitted before 't' and 'p' at the beginning of some words. Examples are:

pwuail	*spoil*
tan-op	*stand up*
tik	*stick*

Long 'O' Sound

When the long English 'o' sound (even when represented by 'ou' and 'oa') occurs between two consonants, it is frequently replaced by 'uo'. Examples include:

buot	*boat*
guol	*gold*
kuot	*court*
suoda	*soda*

'A' Sound

When the long English 'a' (pronounced like the *a* in gate) occurs between two consonants, it is frequently replaced by 'ye'. Examples are:

fyet	*fate*
gyet	*gate*
lyet	*late*

When the sharp English 'a' (pronounced like *a* in car) occurs after 'c' or 'k' and before another consonant, it is frequently replaced with 'ya' (when the word has one syllable) and 'yaa' (when the word has more than one syllable). Examples are:

kyaad	*card*
kyaar	*car*
kyabij	*cabbage*
kyatapilla	*caterpillar*

B Replaces V

For emphasis, 'b' is sometimes used to replace 'v'. Some examples are:

ebridyeh	*everyday*
ebriweh	*everywhere*
riba	*river*

Omitting and Adding 'H'

Some Jamaicans omit the *h* at the beginning of words, for example, pronouncing *head* as *ed*. Some Jamaicans add an *h* to words beginning with a vowel, for example, pronouncing *all* as *hall*.

"W" is sometimes omitted or replaced with an 'h' before the 'u' sound at the beginning of a word (even when represented by 'oo' or 'ou'). For example, when 'h' is omitted *wood*, *would*, and *woman* become *ud*, *ud*, and *uhman* in Jamaican Creole. When an 'h' replaces 'w,' they become *hud*, *hud*, and *huhman*, respectively.

When Kk'l, K'l, Gg'l, and G'l Replace Ttl, Tl, Ddl, and Dl

'Ttl' and 'tl' are sometimes replaced by 'kk'l' and 'k'l', respectively. Examples are:

jengk'l	*gentle*
likk'l	*little*

'Ddl' and 'dl' are sometimes replaced by 'gg'l' and 'g'l', respectively. Examples are:

figg'l	*fiddle*
kyang'l	*candle*

The Article Di

In Jamaican Creole, the definite article *di* (E. *the*) is omitted when mentioning non-specific nouns. The English language does this inconsistently, but Jamaican Creole consistently uses this rule.

A **non-specific noun** is a noun that refers to a general class of people, places, animals, or things as opposed to a specific person, place, animal, or thing from that group.

For example:

Jamaican Creole	English
Wi goh a <u>mall</u>.	We go to <u>the mall</u>.
Shi goh a <u>wok</u>.	She goes to <u>work</u>.
Yuh goh a <u>club</u>.	You go to [the] <u>club</u>.

The Use of There

While sentences in English can begin with the word *there*, a sentence is never started with *dyer* or *deh* (E. *there*) in Jamaican Creole. For example, you will never hear a Jamaican say: *Dyer a nobody ya* (E. *There is nobody here*). Instead, the sentence would be constructed: *Nobody noh deh ya* (E. *Nobody is here*).

Practice Exercise 1

Put the skills you have learned to test by pronouncing the following words. You should also try to figure out the English meaning.

anti	winda	bredda	fishaman
tik	madda	wi	granfaada
neva	wyeh	waata	haat

Practice Exercise 2

Write the English translation for the following words.

aatifishal   _____

gryet   _____

kip   _____

matta   _____

pyeh   _____

rispan   _____

sinting   _____

suoda   _____

tek   _____

wa   _____

Practice Exercise 3

Match the following Jamaican Creole words with the English meaning on the right by drawing a line.

barro	catapult
duo	snow
faama	most
gyada	snore
kyatapol	borrow
kyeta	gather
muos	door
sinuor	farmer
sinuo	weather
wedda	cater

Practice Exercise 4

Identify the Jamaican Creole word in the following sentences. Write the word on the line.

1. Kadeen had put the pikcha on the wall. _____
2. The man siniiz. _____
3. Tomorrow is the first dyeh of the new year, and it is my father's birthday. _____
4. My grandmother likes to drink gyaalic tea every morning. _____
5. Omar expek to pass his English exam with flying colors. _____
6. In the migg'l of the square, there was a manument of the hero. _____
7. They huop that the bus will not be delayed, or they will miss their flight. _____
8. The woman has put a lot of wok into the project. _____
9. The little boy huol the door open for the woman. _____
10. The workers dimaan a raise in pay from their employers. _____

Practice Exercise 5

Write the English word for each Jamaican Creole word you identified in Practice Exercise 4. Write the English word on the line. If the word is a verb, be sure to use the correct form of the verb.

1. Kadeen had put the pikcha on the wall. _____
2. The man siniiz. _____
3. Tomorrow is the first dyeh of the new year, and it is my father's birthday. _____

4. My grandmother likes to drink gyaalic tea every morning.
   _____

5. Omar expek to pass his English exam with flying colors.
   _____

6. In the migg'l of the square, there was a manument of the hero.
   _____

7. They huop that the bus will not be delayed, or they will miss their flight. _____

8. The woman has put lot of wok into the project. _____

9. The little boy huol the door open for the woman.
   _____

10. The workers dimaan a raise in pay from their employers.
    _____

Practice Exercise 6

Look at the following words. Write the English translation on the line. The parts of speech of each word are written to help you determine the English translation.

aweh *adv.* _____   **jangcro** *n.* _____
datdeh *adj., pron.* _____   **nyeli** *adv.* _____
faam *n., v.* _____   **ong'l** *adj., adv.* _____
indeh *contr.* _____   **yasso** *adv., n.* _____

Pluralizing

The part of speech of a word determines how it is pluralized. The pluralization of adjectives, nouns, and pronouns is discussed in this lesson.

Pluralizing Indefinite Adjectives and Adjectives of Quantity

Most of the indefinite adjectives and adjectives of quantity that are used in English are also used in Jamaican Creole. Indefinite adjectives and adjectives of quantity have no plural form in English or Jamaican Creole.

> **Indefinite adjectives** are formed from indefinite pronouns and describe a quality or quantity of that noun or pronoun in a non-specific way. Examples of indefinite adjectives include E. *few*, E. *some*, and E. *many*.

> **Adjectives of quantity** give an estimation of the amount or quantity of a noun or pronoun. Examples of adjectives of quantity include E. *ten*, E. *five*, and E. *one*.

For example:

Jamaican Creole	English
<u>Nof</u> a dem nuo.	<u>A lot</u> of them know.
<u>One</u> chance im a get.	lit. <u>One</u> chance he is getting.
	(He is getting one chance.)
<u>Six</u> kyang'l a bon.	<u>Six</u> candles are burning.

Pluralizing Demonstrative Adjectives

The demonstrative adjectives of Jamaican Creole are *da, dis, disya, dat,* and *datdeh.* The demonstrative adjectives of English are *this* and *that.*

> **Demonstrative adjectives** let us know what specific thing, place, or person is being referred to.

They are pluralized as follows:

Singular	English	Plural	English
da/dis/disya	this	demya	these
da/dat/datdeh	that	demdeh	those

(The uses of da, dat, and datdeh are discussed later).

Examples of the use of demonstrative adjectives:

Jamaican Creole	English
<u>Demya</u> dress look di syem.	<u>These</u> dresses look the same.
Im a move <u>demdeh</u> furniture out a di wyeh.	He is moving <u>those</u> furniture out of the way.
<u>Demya</u> pikni belong inna class two.	<u>These</u> children belong in class two.

Differentiating the Meanings of Da

Da can be used in Jamaican Creole to mean *this* or *that*. To differentiate between *this* and *that*, the pronouns *deh*, *dyer*, and *ya* are placed after the noun referred to by *da*. *Dehsoh*, *dyersoh*, and *yasso* are also used, but to a lesser extent.

Jamaican Creole Word	English Meaning
deh	there
dyer	there
ya	here
dehsoh	there, right there
dyersoh	there, right there
yasso	here, right here

The meaning of *da* when used with *deh*, *dyer*, *ya*, etc.:

Adjective	Used With	Meaning
da	deh, dyer, dehsoh, dyersoh	that
da	ya, yasso	this

Here are some examples of the use of *da*:

Jamaican Creole	English
<u>Da</u> kyaar <u>ya</u> ha wau dent inna di side.	<u>This</u> car <u>here</u> has a dent in the side.
Melissa move <u>da</u> toy <u>deh</u> off di tyeb'l.	Melissa moved <u>that</u> toy <u>there</u> off the table.
<u>Da</u> bag <u>yasso</u> belong inna di closet.	<u>This</u> bag <u>right here</u> belongs in the closet.

When Deh, Dyer, and Ya Are Used with Disya, Datdeh, and Demya

Deh, *dyer*, and *ya* are sometimes used with a noun after *disya*, *datdeh*, *demya*, and *demdeh*. This is done to show a specific location or for emphasis. *Dehsoh*, *dyersoh*, and *yasso* are also used.

The meaning of *disya*, *datdeh*, *demya*, and *demdeh* when used with *deh*, *dyer*, and *ya*:

Adjective	Used With	Meaning	Describes
disya	ya, yasso	this here	a thing close to the subject.
demya	ya, yasso	these here	some things close to the subject.
datdeh	deh, dyer, dehsoh, dyersoh	that there	a thing at a distance from the subject.
demdeh	deh, dyer, dehsoh, dyersoh	those there	some things at a distance from the subject.

For example:

Jamaican Creole	English
<u>Demya</u> blouse <u>yasso</u> ha huol inna dem.	<u>These</u> blouses <u>right here</u> have holes in them.
*Wi tink bout <u>demdeh</u> tings <u>deh.</u>	We think about <u>those</u> things <u>there</u>.
Put <u>disya</u> one <u>ya</u> pan di shelf.	Put <u>this</u> one <u>here</u> on the shelf.

* When used in this way, deh does not refer to a literal place. It is used for emphasis in this example. Dehsoh and dyersoh always refer to a literal place.

When Disya, Datdeh, Demya, and Demdeh Are Shortened

In some cases, *disya*, *datdeh*, *demya*, and *demdeh* are shortened to *dis*, *dat*, *dem*, and *dem*. These are cases where *deh*, *dyer*, *dehsoh*, *dyersoh*, *ya*, and *yasso* are used after the noun. This does not change the meaning of the sentence. For example:

Jamaican Creole	English
<u>Dem</u> blouse <u>dehsoh</u> ha huol inna dem.	<u>Those</u> blouses <u>right there</u> have holes in them.
Wi tink bout <u>dem</u> tings <u>deh.</u>	We think about <u>those</u> things <u>there</u>.
Put <u>dis</u> one <u>ya</u> pan di shelf.	Put <u>this</u> one <u>here</u> on the shelf.

Pluralizing Adjectives Demonstrating Possession

The following table outlines the pluralization of possessive adjectives.

> **Adjectives demonstrating possession** (demonstrative adjectives) show the relationship between two things, two people, or a person and a thing. They show how one is owned or possessed by the other.

Possessive Adjectives

Person	Singular	English	Plural	English
First	mi/fimmi	my	wi/fiwi	our
Second	yuh/fiyuh	your	unnu/fiunnu/ fuunu	your
Third	iih/im/fihim	his	deeh/dem/fidem	their
Second (plural)	aar/fiar	her	deeh/dem/fidem	their
Third (plural)	ih/fiit/fihit	its	deeh/dem/fidem	their

(Adjectives demonstrating possession will be discussed later).

Pluralizing Nouns

In English, nouns are pluralized by quantity, and 's' or 'es' is added to the noun (except certain nouns that are not changed in the plural, such as sheep, deer, or furniture, etc.) or those that occur in the the plural form (such as scissors, pants, etc.).

> A **noun** refers to a person, place, animal, or thing.

Here are examples of English nouns and their plurals:

Singular	Plural	Singular	Plural
girl	girls	cloud	clouds
dish	dishes	fish	fish/fishes
mail	mail	monkey	monkeys
tree	trees	mango	mangoes

Pluralizing Nouns in Jamaican Creole

In Jamaican Creole, a noun is pluralized depending on the quantity of the noun and whether it is specific or non-specific.

Specific Nouns

Specific nouns that are of a quantity greater than one are pluralized by adding *dem* (E. *them*) after the noun.

> A **specific noun** refers to a particular noun that is modified by the definite article (E. *the*), an adjective demonstrating possession, or another noun demonstrating possession (for example, *the pencils, our lunches,* and *Keisha's houses*).

Here are some examples of the use of specific nouns in the plural form:

Jamaican Creole	English
Di tiicha dem deh pan strike.	The teachers are on strike.
*Patsy daag dem deh inna di yaad.	Patsy's dogs are in the yard.
*Aar kyaar dem run good.	Her cars run good/well.

(Showing ownership is discussed later).

Non-specific Nouns

Non-specific nouns are not pluralized regardless of quantity. If a non-specific noun is used, it signals that the speaker is not concerned about quantity.

A **non-specific noun** refers to a general class or group of nouns (*pencils*, *lunches*, and *houses*).

For example:

Jamaican Creole	English
Tiicha deh pan strike.	Teachers are on strike.
Daag deh inna di yaad.	Dogs are in the yard.
kyaar run good.	Cars run good/well.

Noun Phrases with Plural Adjectives

Noun phrases that include an adjective that suggests that the noun is plural do not require *dem* to form their plural. Examples are *nof, muo,* and *five* (E. *a lot, more,* and *five*). The plural adjective automatically makes the noun phrase plural. This makes using *dem* unnecessary. For example:

Jamaican Creole	English
Nof people a come a di fyer.	Plenty people are coming to the fair.
Five chicken inna di cub.	Five chickens are in the coop.
Demdeh riva deh dry muo time.	Those rivers are dry sometimes.

There are a few exceptions to the above rules, however, with words like *iyer* and *ting* being pluralized *iyers/iyerz* (E. *years*) and *tings/tingz* (E. *things*), except when the noun is being used as a specific noun. In this case, *dem* is added.

An example of *tingz* being used in a specific manner:

Di tingz dem deh ya (E. *The things are here*).

An example of *tingz* being used in a non-specific manner:

Tingz good (E. *Things are good*).

Nouns with an Irregular Plural Form

Certain plural nouns that are irregular in English (such as *people*, *furniture*, and *fish*) are not pluralized by adding *dem* in Jamaican Creole when used as non-specific nouns. They are always pluralized by adding *dem* when used as specific nouns.

Consider the following examples:

People love di prime minista (E. *People love the prime minister*).

Di people dem a protes (E. *The people are protesting*).

In the second example, *people* is used as a specific noun. Nouns that mainly occur in the plural form, such as *shoes, pants*, etc., are used in Jamaican Creole as they are in English except when used as specific nouns, in which case *dem* is used after the noun.

For example:

Shoes fi wear outside (E. *Shoes should be worn outside*).

Di shoes dem uol (E. *The shoes are old*).

Nouns That Follow Plural Pronouns or Nouns

A noun that follows a plural pronoun or a noun that has already been pluralized by adding *dem* is not pluralized. The noun is either used as a non-specific noun, or an adjective that indicates the amount of the noun (e.g. *nof* (E. *plenty*)) is added. For example:

Jamaican Creole	English
*Di pikni dem ha book.	The children have books.
Di pikni dem ha ten book.	The children have ten books.
Dem a coz'n.	They are cousins.

It can be assumed that the specific number of books that the children have is not important to the speaker. If it were, the speaker would have explicitly stated the number.

If a noun or noun phrase has been pluralized with *dem* and a second noun or noun phrase includes a specific noun, the second noun or noun phrase is usually made plural by adding *dem*. For example:

Jamaican Creole	English
<u>Di byeliff dem</u> tek <u>di kyaar dem</u> an <u>di book dem</u>.	<u>The bailiffs</u> took <u>the cars</u> and <u>the books</u>.
*<u>Mi fren dem</u> gi <u>fidem pikni dem</u> mango.	<u>My friends</u> give <u>their children</u> mangoes.
<u>Di employee dem</u> like all a <u>di manija dem</u> weh dem wok wid.	<u>The employees</u> like all of <u>the managers</u> that they work with.

Note in the second example that mango is not pluralized in Jamaican Creole. This is because mangoes are a general category of nouns, and the mangoes mentioned are referred to in a nonspecific way.

People Who Fall into the Same Category

If a speaker wishes to communicate that two or more people fall into the same category, this is communicated by mentioning the name of one of those two persons or the names of a few persons from the group and adding *dem*. For example:

Jamaican Creole	English
<u>Kenisha dem</u> a goh a Kingston.	<u>Kenisha [and the others]</u> are going to Kingston.
<u>Maas Kenny an Miss Judy dem</u> a family.	<u>Mr. Kenny and Miss Judy [and the others]</u> are family.
Wi did nuo <u>Will dem</u>.	We knew <u>Will [and the others]</u>.

Pluralizing Personal Pronouns

There are four types of personal pronouns.

> A **personal pronoun** takes the place of a noun (person, place, animal, or thing).

The personal pronouns are pluralized as follows:

Subject Personal Pronouns

Singular	English	Plural	English
mi	I	wi	we
yuh	you	unnu	you
iih/im	he	dem/deeh	they
shi	she	dem/deeh	they
ih/E. it	it	dem/deeh	they

Object Personal Pronouns

Singular	English	Plural	English
mi	me	wi	us
yuh	you	unnu	you
im/E. him	him	dem	them
*aar/E. she	her	dem	them
ih/E. it	it	dem	them

*E. *She* is frequently used instead of *aar* following the regular present conjugation of the verb *bi*, e.g., *A she* (E. *It is she*).

*Possessive Personal Pronouns

Singular	English	Plural	English
fimmi	mine	fiwi	ours
fiyuh	yours	fuunu/fiunnu	yours
fihim	his	fidem	theirs
fiar	hers	fidem	theirs
fiit/fihit	its	fidem	theirs

*(*The use of possessive pronouns is discussed later*).

28

Reflexive Personal Pronouns

Singular	English	Plural	English
miself	myself	wiself	ourselves
yuhself	yourself	unnuself	yourselves
iihself/imself	himself	deehself/ demself	themselves
aarself	herself	deehself/ demself	themselves
ihself	itself	deehself/ demself	themselves

The pronouns previously listed are used in a similar manner in Jamaican Creole as they are in English. For example:

Jamaican Creole	English
<u>Deeh</u> did duh di wok.	<u>They</u> had done the work.
<u>Wi</u> fix di problem <u>wiself</u>.	<u>We</u> fixed the problem <u>ourselves</u>.
<u>Unnu</u> a run out a time.	<u>You</u> are running out of time.
Lef <u>dem</u> aluon.	Leave <u>them</u> alone.

Pluralizing Demonstrative Pronouns

The demonstrative pronouns of English are *this* and *that*. They are sometimes used in place of demonstrative adjectives. For example, instead of using the phrase *this bag*, the demonstrative pronoun *this* can be used in its place if it is understood that the bag is being referred to.

> The **demonstrative pronoun** is a type of pronoun that is used in place of the demonstrative adjective.

In Jamaican Creole, the demonstrative pronouns are *dis, disya, dat,* and *datdeh.* They are pluralized as follows:

Singular	English	Plural	English
dis/disya	this	demya	these
dat/datdeh	that	demdeh	those

Some examples of the use of demonstrative pronouns include:

Jamaican Creole	English
<u>Demya</u> did get wet.	<u>These</u> got wet.
Mi like <u>disya</u>.	I like <u>this</u>.
<u>Demdeh</u> a ton yellow.	<u>Those</u> are turning yellow.

Pluralizing Indefinite Pronouns

Indefinite pronouns exist in either a plural or a singular form. Examples of indefinite pronouns include E. *some*, E. *much*, and E. *few*. These words have no plural form in English or Jamaican Creole. Most of the indefinite pronouns that are used in English are also used in Jamaican Creole.

> An **indefinite pronoun** stands for a nonspecific thing, place, animal, or person.

For example:

Jamaican Creole	English
<u>Some</u> expek wi fi fyel.	<u>Some</u> expect us to fail.
Im gi im son <u>plenty</u>.	He gives his son <u>plenty</u>.
Etta seh goodbye to <u>all</u>.	Etta said goodbye to <u>all</u>.

Practice Exercise 7

Translate the following sentences to Jamaican Creole.

1. The students are playing in the schoolyard.

    _____

2. We will visit the museum next summer.

    _____

3. My cousin likes pears and apples.

    _____

4. They are from St. Mary, but they live in Kingston.

    _____

5. Our pets spread the rubbish around the yard.

    _____

6. Five boys and six girls are on the debate team.

    _____

7. My coworkers will be working for an hour later than usual this evening.

    _____

8. The birds flew from tree to tree.

    _____

9. Lisa, Tina, and company shop at the store every Saturday.

    _____

10. All businesses are closed today because of the holiday.

    _____

Practice Exercise 8

Translate the following sentences to English.

1. Di pikni dem ^{E}believe inna ^{E}magic.

    _____

2. Wi pyeh fi wi tex$_E$book dem frau laas mont.

    _____

3. Shiela ᴶdem always exercise ᴶpau Sunday.

    _____

4. ᴱTen ᴱmango jap aaf a di ᴱtree.

    _____

5. Di kyaar dem pyent inna ᴱred an ᴱyellow.

    _____

6. ᴱAll a di ᴱshop dem cluos pau ᴱSaturday.

    _____

7. Dem ha nof ᴱtree inna dem yaad.

    _____

8. Mi ha ᴱfive muo chapta fi ᴱread inna mi ᴱEnglish tex_ᴱbook.

    _____

9. Mi fren dem naah goh a ᴱschool fi ᴱtwo dyeh.

    _____

10. ᴶIm cash two check ᴶa ᴶdi bank.

    _____

Practice Exercise 9

Identify and underline the plural word/s or phrase/s in the following Jamaican Creole sentences.

1. Dem seh dem aggo gi wi fuon ᴱcredit fi ᴱcall wi madda.
2. ᴱDaniesha an aar granmadda ᴱput ᴱup di dekaryeshan dem pan di ᴱwall.
3. Mi ha ᴱtwo ᴱblue sweta auh wau ᴱblack ᴱone fi ᴱwear goh a ᴱschool.
4. ᴱRose ᴱput demya ᴱbanana ya pan di tyeb'l fi yuh.
5. Di ᴱpeople dem ᴱbuy ᴱall a di ᴱfood dem inna di ᴱstore bikaah di ᴱhurricane a ᴱcome.

6. ᴱFour ᴱbus inna di paak, ᴱbut dem a goh a ᴱOcho ᴱRios, an mi a goh a ᴱMontego ᴱBay.

7. Di ᴱbreeze bluo dong di ᴱtree dem inna di yaad an mash-op di gyaad'n.

8. Two big movie ᴶa come out ᴶinna ᴶdi ᴶsamma.

9. ᴱSheena tek ᴱtwo ᴱpill fi aar head ᴶiyek an aggo tek ᴱtwo muo inna wau likk'l ᴱwhile.

10. Di bwuay ha ᴱtwo fuon pau ᴱtwo diffrent ᴱnetwork.

Practice Exercise 10

Translate the sentences from Practice Exercise 9 to English. Write each sentence on the line.

1. _____
2. _____
3. _____
4. _____
5. _____
6. _____
7. _____
8. _____
9. _____
10. _____

Practice Exercise 11

Translate and pluralize the following sentences in Jamaican Creole. All words that can be pluralized should be pluralized. Write each sentence on the line.

1. The girl took the book that she borrowed to the library.

_____

2. The door is open.

   _____

3. Damion is taking a water bottle and snack with him on the trip.

   _____

4. A candle is burning in the room.

   _____

5. He needs more time to finish the exam.

   _____

6. The nurse is attending to the sick patient at the hospital.

   _____

7. There is a car making its way along the highway.

   _____

8. The keyboard on the laptop is broken and needs to be fixed.

   _____

9. The teacher is meeting with the principal of the school.

   _____

10. She will put all her money in the bank.

   _____

Practice Exercise 12

Use the following words to form plural sentences in Jamaican Creole. Identify the part of speech of the word you used by writing it on the line (e.g. noun, verb, etc.).

ancaal-fa *adj.* uncalled-for
iyer *n.* year
kaapet/kyaapet *n., v.* carpet
muo *adj., adv., pron.* more

pakit *adj., n., v.* pocket
washi *adj.* weak
ramp *v.* play

1. _____

   Part of speech _____

2. _____

   Part of speech _____

3. _____

   Part of speech _____

4. _____

   Part of speech _____

5. _____

   Part of speech _____

6. _____

   Part of speech _____

7. _____

   Part of speech _____

When a Verb Phrase Contains an Infinitive Verb

In English, the infinitive form of a verb is the verb used along with *to*. An example of an infinitive verb is *to leave*. Here are some examples of infinitive verbs used in English sentences:

They have to know how to handle the matter.

Kadeen is going to write the letters today.

To make it on time, he will have to hurry.

In Jamaican Creole, the infinitive verb combines *fi* and the base infinitive form of the verb. An example of this is *fi run* (E. *to run*).

> The **base infinitive form** of a verb is when the verb is used without adding *to* (an example of this is *know* which differs from the **infinitive form** *to know*).

Here are some examples of infinitive verbs with their English meaning:

Jamaican Creole	English
Trevor a come <u>fi si</u> im fren.	Trevor is coming <u>to see</u> his friend.
Wi aggo ha <u>fi lef</u>.	We will have <u>to leave</u>.
Di store uona a wyet <u>fi aada</u> stock.	The store owner is waiting <u>to order</u> stock.

Infinitives and the Verb Bi

The verb *bi* is never used before an infinitive verb. Jamaicans would state the sentence in a manner that avoids this formation. For example, the sentence *Bobby is to take the exam soon* might be stated *Bobby aggo tek di exam soon* (E. *Bobby will take the exam soon*).

The verb *bi* behaves regularly in all other instances and is used in its infinitive form after another verb (except when used before adjectives and prepositions as discussed later). For example:

Jamaican Creole	English
Sue-Sue <u>preten fi bi</u> taiyad.	Sue-Sue <u>pretends to be</u> tired.
Teresa <u>wau yuh fi bi</u> aar bridesmaid.	Teresa <u>wants you to be</u> her bridesmaid.
Yanique <u>a study fi bi</u> wau dacta.	Yanique <u>is studying to be</u> a doctor.

Prepositions and the Verb Fi Bi

The verb *fi bi* (E. *to be*) is irregular when used directly before prepositions such as *a, pau, pan, inna, oova, anda, dong, agens, afta,* and *aaf,* and adverbs such as *ya, deh, dyer* that indicate position or location and becomes *fi deh* when used before them. In most instances, the sentence is stating the physical location or position of the subject.

The following prepositions and adverbs indicate position or location:

Preposition	English Meaning	Adverb	English Meaning
a	at	ya	here
pau	on	deh	there
pan	on	dyer	there
inna	in		
oova	over		
anda	under		
dong	down		
agens	against		

Preposition	English Meaning	Adverb	English Meaning
afta	after		
aaf	off		

Here are some examples of the verb when used with the previous prepositions and adverbs:

Jamaican Creole	English
Mi <u>huop fi deh a</u> mi yaad pan di halidyeh.	I <u>hope to be at</u> my home on the holiday.
Simone <u>wau fi deh pan</u> di team.	Simone <u>wants to be on</u> the team.
Misha <u>a expek fi deh</u> a Hanover tomorrow.	Misha <u>is expecting to be</u> in Hanover tomorrow.

Despite this general rule, speakers of Jamaican Creole sometimes omit the verb before prepositions such as *inna, oova, anda, dong, agens, afta,* and *aaf. Fi* is still used before the preposition, however.

For example:

Jamaican Creole	English
Lenny <u>wau fi inna</u> di fos group.	Lenny <u>wants to be</u> in the first group.
Dem <u>expek fi afta</u> aar.	They <u>expect to be after</u> her.
Ih <u>seem fi oova</u> arredi.	It <u>seems to [be] over</u> already.

Fi deh is always used before *a, pan, pau, deh, dyer,* and *ya.* For example:

Jamaican Creole	English
Shelly <u>wau fi deh a</u> wok pan time.	Shelly <u>wants to be at</u> work on time.
Gina <u>huop fi deh deh.</u>	Gina <u>hopes to be there.</u>
Wi <u>ha fi deh pan</u> wi wyeh soon.	We <u>have to be on</u> our way soon.

Adjectives and the Verb Fi Bi

The verb *fi bi* can either be used or omitted when it occurs in its infinitive form before an adjective. *Fi* (E. *to*) is used before the adjective even if the verb is omitted. For example:

Jamaican Creole	English
Dem <u>ha fi naive</u> fi believe dat.	lit. They <u>have to naive</u> to believe that.
	(They have to be naive to believe that.)
Di ruop <u>seem fi bi strong</u>.	The rope <u>seems to be strong</u>.
Everybody <u>wish fi happy</u>.	lit. Everybody <u>wishes to happy</u>.
	(Everybody wishes to be happy.)

If an adverb modifies the adjective, the previous rule is still followed. Examples of adverbs include *rather, slowly,* and *there.*

> An **adverb** is a word that modifies a verb, adjective, or another adverb. It can give information about the manner in which an action is done. It can also indicate time, place, or extent.

Here are some examples:

Jamaican Creole	English
Di ruop <u>seem fi bi **very** strong</u>.	The ruop <u>seems to be **very** strong</u>.
Dem <u>ha fi **really** naive</u> fi believe dat.	lit. They <u>have to **really** naive</u> to believe that.
	(They have to be really naive to believe that.)
Everybody <u>wish fi **totally** happy</u>.	lit. Everybody <u>wishes to **totally** happy</u>.
	(Everybody wishes to be totally happy.)

When an adjective describes nationality, the verb is always used in its infinitive form. For example:

Jamaican Creole	English
Jerome <u>wish fi bi</u> Guyanese.	Jerome <u>wishes to be</u> Guyanese.
Im <u>seem fi bi</u> Jamaican.	He <u>seems to be</u> Jamaican.

Infinitive Verbs Used after the Verb Goh

When an infinitive verb occurs after the verb *goh* (E. *go*) in the continuous present tense, the continuous past tense, the future tense, and the conditional future tense, the infinitive verb becomes irregular. In these cases, the verb is used in its base infinitive form instead of its infinitive form. For example:

The Continuous Present Tense

Jamaican Creole	English
Di byebi <u>a goh sleep</u>.	The baby <u>is going [to] sleep</u>.
Trina <u>a goh pick</u> wau flowaz.	Trina <u>is going [to] pick</u> a flower.
Pam <u>a goh goh</u> a school.	Pam <u>is going [to] go</u> to school.

The Continuous Past Tense

Jamaican Creole	English
Clive dem <u>did a goh wash</u> di kyaar.	Clive [and others] <u>were going [to] wash</u> the car.
Leroy <u>did a goh goh</u> a May Pen.	Leroy <u>was going [to] go</u> to May Pen.
Di student dem <u>did a goh study</u>.	The students <u>were going [to] study</u>.

The Future Tense

Jamaican Creole	English
Victor <u>a goh goh</u> one dyeh early.	Victor <u>is going [to] go</u> one day early.
Di faiyaman dem <u>gweeh goh help</u> dem.	The firemen <u>will go [to] help</u> them.
Shi <u>a goh aks</u> fi di caas a di item.	She <u>is going ask</u> for the cost of the item.

The Conditional Future Tense

Jamaican Creole	English
Mi <u>wudda goh sleep</u> if mi did deh huom.	I <u>would go [to] sleep</u> if I were home.
Wi <u>wudda goh help</u> dem.	We <u>would go [to] help</u> them.
Aar pikni dem <u>wi goh si</u> aar.	Her children <u>will (possibly) go [to] see</u> her.

Inserting *fi* before the verb that follows *goh* would change the meaning of the sentence. Inserting *fi* after *goh* in the continuous present tense, the continuous past tense, the future tense, and the conditional future tense changes the meaning of *fi* to *in order to*. For example:

Jamaican Creole	English
Wi <u>a goh fi si</u> di mou'n.	We <u>are going in order to see</u> the mountain.
Roy <u>wi goh fi help</u> dem.	Roy <u>will go in order to help</u> them.
Paula <u>a goh</u> a store <u>fi get</u> wau new TV.	Paula <u>is going</u> to [the] store <u>in order to get</u> a new TV.

Infinitive Verbs Used after the Verb Wau

When an infinitive verb follows the verb *wau* (E. *want*), *fi* can either be used or omitted (though it is most times omitted). For example:

Jamaican Creole	English
Yuh madda <u>wau nuo</u> weh yuh deh.	Your mother <u>wants [to] know</u> where you are.
Di pikni dem <u>wau goh</u> wid dem fren.	The children <u>want [to] go</u> with their friends.
Yuh <u>ha fi wau fi succeed</u> fi duh well.	You <u>have to want to succeed</u> to do well.

Practice Exercise 13

Translate the following sentences to Jamaican Creole, and underline the infinitive verb or verbs in each sentence.

1. The manager had to give up his job because he moved to a new city.

    _____

2. We plan to go see the new store on our way to work.

    _____

3. Yanique's mother asked her to close the door on her way out.

    _____

4. To hang the pictures on the wall, we need to put them in picture frames.

    _____

5. They plan to see the show next Christmas.

    _____

6. The tourists went to visit the most famous site in the city.

    _____

7. He wants to be the president of the organization some day.

    _____

8. A plumber will have to fix the leaky faucet.

    _____

9. I am going to cook stewed beef for dinner.

   _____

10. You will have to leave soon in order to catch the bus.

   _____

Practice Exercise 14

Underline the infinitive verb or verbs in the following sentences.

1. Shi ^Elike fi hyeh aar madda ^Esing di ^Esong.
2. Wi iht nof ^Evegetable fi bi ^Ehealthy.
3. Im a goh goh a di baaba ^Eshop pan im wyeh frau ^Eschool.
4. Di pikini dem a staat fi ^Elearn fi ^Eread an ^Ewrite.
5. ^EJerome did goh fi si di dacta, ^Ebut di dacta did ^Eout a di ^Eoffice.
6. Shi did a huop fi mek wau fren inna di ^Egroup.
7. Dem a goh ^Etry fi duh ^Eit inna di maanin.
8. Im a goh ^Ereplace di uol ^Ebulb wid wau ^Enew ^Eone.
9. Di ^Ebike ^Eswerve fi ^Eavoid di puos.
10. Wi wau fi nuo di ^Etruth.

Practice Exercise 15

Translate the sentences from Practice Exercise 14 to English.

1. _____
2. _____
3. _____
4. _____
5. _____
6. _____
7. _____
8. _____

9. _____

10. _____

Practice Exercise 16

Underline the infinitive verb or verbs in the following sentences.

1. ᴶMi ᴶcoz'n like ᴶfi cook rice ᴶan peas ᴶpan Sunday.
2. Deeh wau duh ᴱwell inna dem ᴱexam.
3. Wi a huop fi ᴱfinish di projek pan ᴱtime.
4. Di pikini a goh ᴱsleep ᴱearly.
5. Di ᴱstudent dem did wau fi enta di ᴱcompetition.
6. Wi did a huop fi hyeh di ᴱresult, ᴱbut wi did haffi lef ᴱearly.
7. Di tiicha ha fi ᴱfinish aar ᴱlesson ᴱplan dem ᴱtonight.
8. ᴶIm ᴶwudda like ᴶfi buy ᴶdi shoes ᴶdem, but ᴶdem too expensive.
9. Iih wau fi ᴱfinalize evriting bifuo iih lef di ᴱcountry.
10. Shi a goh a ᴱSt. Thomas fi siim nex ᴱweek.

Practice Exercise 17

Translate the sentences from Practice Exercise 16 to English.

1. _____
2. _____
3. _____
4. _____
5. _____
6. _____
7. _____
8. _____
9. _____
10. _____

Practice Exercise 18

Use the following words to form sentences containing infinitive verbs in Jamaican Creole. Underline the infinitve verb and identify the part of speech of the word you used by writing it on the line (e.g. noun, verb, etc.).

aat *n., v.* art

badbrok *v.* spoilt

egzop *adj.* meddlesome

faama *n.* farmer

galang *interj., v.* go on; behave (in a particular manner)

kyaah *mod. aug., v.* cannot; carry

wamek *adj.* why

1. _____

   Part of speech _____

2. _____

   Part of speech _____

3. _____

   Part of speech _____

4. _____

   Part of speech _____

5. _____

   Part of speech _____

6. _____

   Part of speech _____

7. _____

   Part of speech _____

8. _____

   Part of speech _____

The Passive Voice

The passive voice is being used when the object being acted upon in a sentence is used as the subject of that sentence. This is done to draw attention away from the doer of the action and to award it to the receiver of the action. Usually, there is a combination of the verbs *be*, *have*, or *get* with a past participle of the verb. The active voice, on the other hand, shows how a subject acts upon an object with the subject stated first. Some examples of the passive voice and the active voice of English are:

Passive Voice	Active Voice
The boy is being pushed by his sister.	The boy's sister is pushing him.
He has been seen by the nurse.	The nurse saw him.
They got helped by their friend.	Their friend helped them.

In Jamaican Creole, the verbs *bi* and *ha* are not used before the past participle (as is consistent with the Jamaican Creole present perfect tense), and *get* is only used in rare cases. For example:

Jamaican Creole	English
Di tyeb'l put deh by Jeffrey.	The table [was] put there by Jeffrey.
Wau rat get iht by di cat.	A rat got eaten by the cat.
Di vase brok by di pikni.	The vase [was] broken by the child.

Sometimes the doer of the action is not stated. For example:

Jamaican Creole	English
Di tyeb'l put deh.	The table [was] put there.
Wau rat get iht.	A rat got eaten.
Di vase brok.	The vase [was] broken.

The Impersonal Passive Voice

The impersonal passive voice of English combines the word *it*, the passive voice, and a that-clause. Here are some examples of the impersonal passive voice and how they might be stated in the active voice:

Impersonal Passive Voice	Active Voice
It is expected that he will recover.	We expect that he will recover.
It is known by them that there is no cure.	They know that there is no cure.
It is believed that it might rain today.	They believe it might rain today.

The Impersonal Passive Voice of Jamaican Creole

Jamaican Creole also uses the impersonal passive voice by placing *a* (E. *it is*) or *a did/a beeh/a weeh/a beeh did/a weeh did* (E. *it was*) at the beginning of the sentence. The phrase that a person uses depends on which parish of Jamaica they are from.

The impersonal passive voice of Jamaican Creole is used for two reasons. The first reason is to draw attention to some part of the sentence, such as the subject, object acted upon, the action done, or an adjective describing the subject. The second reason is to respond to questions. The part of the sentence that attention is drawn to depends on what needs to be emphasized. The conjunction *dat* and the pronoun *who* are usually omitted in these sentences.

Drawing Attention to the Subject of a Sentence

Jamaicans draw attention to the subject of a sentence by placing *a* or *a did* (also used as *a beeh, a weeh, a beeh did,* or *a weeh did*) before the subject noun or pronoun that is being emphasized. *A did, a beeh, a weeh, a beeh did,* and *a weeh did* indicate that the event or action took place in the past, even if other verbs in the predicate are used in the present tense. Similarly, even if *a* is used at the beginning of the Jamaican Creole sentence, verbs used in the past tense in the predicate would make the entire sentence past. In English, however, all verbs are used in the past tense if all events took place in the past.

Let us imagine that someone did something wrong, and you were being blamed for it. You want it to be known that it was Sharon who did the bad thing. Instead of simply saying *Sharon did dwiit,* most people would say *A Sharon did dwiit* (E. *It was Sharon [who] did it*). The emphasis is thus placed on Sharon. For example:

Jamaican Creole	English
A did di man cut di grass yessideh.	It was the man [that] cut the grass yesterday.
A Jerome a goh goh pan di trip.	It is Jerome [who] is going to go on the trip.
A beeh mi fren gi him twenty dalla fi im fyer.	It was my friend [who] gave him twenty dollars for his fare.

Drawing Attention to the Noun or Pronoun That Is Not the Subject of a Sentence

Jamaicans draw attention to a noun or pronoun that is not the subject of the sentence by placing *a* or *a did,* etc., before the noun or pronoun being emphasized at the beginning of the sentence. For example:

Jamaican Creole	English
A beeh did yessideh di man cut di grass.	It was yesterday [that] the man cut the grass.
A di trip Jerome a goh goh pan.	It is the trip [that] Jerome is going to go on.

Jamaican Creole	English
<u>A did him</u> mi fren did gi twenty dalla fi im fyer.	<u>It was he</u> [whom] my friend gave twenty dollars for his fare.

In the previous three sentences, *the man*, *Jerome*, and *my friend* are the subjects of the sentences. The sentences were reconstructed, however, to draw attention to *yesterday*, *the trip*, and *he*.

Drawing Attention to the Subject's Action

If Jamaicans wish to draw attention to the subject's action, then the sentence is reconstructed so that the verb that describes the action being emphasized is stated first. This format of the passive voice is not used in English. Jamaicans construct these sentences in two ways:

1. *A* or *a did*, etc., is placed before the verb describing the action being emphasized at the beginning of the sentence. This verb will also be repeated in the predicate of the sentence, although the tense might change to show when the action takes place. If it is part of a sentence with multiple verbs, it is usually the first verb mentioned. As stated before, *a did* indicates that the event or action took place in the past, even if other verbs in the predicate are used in the present tense. For example:

Jamaican Creole	English
<u>A ryek</u> im did a ryek di leaf dem inna di yaad.	<u>lit. It is rake</u> [that] he was raking the leaves in the yard.
	(He was raking the leaves in the yard.)
<u>A come</u> dem did a come.	<u>lit. It is come</u> [that] they were coming.
	(They were coming.)
<u>A weeh did sing</u> shi a sing an dance when shi fall dong.	<u>lit. It was sing</u> [that] she was singing and dancing when she fell down.
	(She was singing and dancing when she fell down.)

As you can see in the previous sentences, the verb is used as if it is the subject of the sentence.

2. The verb that describes the action being emphasized is placed at the beginning of the sentence and is also used in the predicate of the sentence. In this case *a* or *a did*, etc., is not placed before the verb. The verb is used in its base infinitive form regardless of the tense it will take in the predicate of the sentence. It would appear that this version is just an abbreviation of the previous construction. For example:

Jamaican Creole	English
<u>Ryek</u> im did a ryek di leaf dem inna di yaad.	lit. <u>Rake</u> [that] he was raking the leaves in the yard.
	(He was raking the leaves in the yard.)
<u>Come</u> dem did a come.	lit. <u>Come</u> [that] they were coming.
	(They were coming.)
<u>Sing</u> shi did a sing an dance when shi fall dong.	lit. <u>Sing</u> [that] she was singing and dancing when she fell down.
	(She was singing and dancing when she fell down.)

Drawing Attention to an Adjective Describing a Subject

The passive voice that draws attention to an adjective is used in Jamaican Creole, but it is not used in English. If one wants to emphasize an adjective describing the subject, then one of two things can be done:

1. *A* or *a did*, etc., is placed before the adjective that describes the subject at the beginning of the sentence. This is one of the rare instances where the verb *bi* is used before an adjective in a Jamaican Creole sentence. This adjective will also be repeated in the predicate of the Jamaican Creole sentence. Notice, however, that the verb *bi* is absent in the predicate. If more than one adjective describe the subject, the first adjective is usually the one emphasized. For example:

Jamaican Creole	English
A <u>ridiculous</u> ih ridiculous.	lit. <u>It is ridiculous</u> [that] it is ridiculous.
	(It is ridiculous.)
A <u>beeh did sorry</u> shi sorry.	lit. <u>It was sorry</u> [that] she was sorry.
	(She was sorry.)
A <u>sleepy</u> di byebi weeh sleepy auh taiyad.	lit. <u>It is sleepy</u> [that] the baby was sleepy and tired.
	(The baby was sleepy and tired.)

2. The adjective can also be used at the beginning of the sentence and is repeated in the predicate. *A* and *a did*, etc., are not used at the beginning of the sentence. This formation is an abbreviation of the previous construction. For example:

Jamaican Creole	English
<u>Ridiculous</u> ih ridiculous.	lit. <u>Ridiculous</u> [that] it is ridiculous.
	(It is ridiculous.)
<u>Sorry</u> shi beeh sorry.	lit. <u>Sorry</u> [that] she was sorry.
	(She was sorry.)
<u>Sleepy</u> di byebi weeh sleepy auh taiyad.	lit. <u>Sleepy</u> [that] the baby was sleepy and tired.
	(The baby was sleepy and tired.)

Practice Exercise 19

Translate the following sentences to Jamaican Creole.

1. It was the dog that chased after the cat.

   _____

2. It is courage that is needed to make it to the end.

   _____

3. His finger got burned by the hot stove.

   _____

4. The family got wet by the rain.

   _____

5. Anancy got tricked by the cunning cat.

   _____

6. The bird was blown over the hibiscus hedging by the wind.

   _____

7. It is expected that they will arrive soon.

   _____

8. The grass got trampled by the galloping horses.

   _____

9. The house was flooded by the river.

   _____

10. Her clothes got torn by the thorny bushes.

    _____

Practice Exercise 20

Translate the following sentences to English.

1. A [E]five a dem inna di [E]office a wyet pan di manija fi
   [E]come [E]back.

   _____

2. Di tyeb'l [E]get brok [E]by di pikini dem weh did a plyeh inna di
   [E]dining [E]room.

   _____

3. Di waata [E]get dashweh pan di [E]floor.

   _____

4. A did yessideh wi ^Eget huom frau wi ^Etrip ^Eto ^ETrinidad.

_____

5. ^JDi food ^Jdid get cook by ^Jmi ^Jfaada.

_____

6. A di fuon ^EKerry did deh pan ^Ewhen wi a lef.

_____

7. Di kyek did iht ^Eby ^EKemar.

_____

8. ^EHappy dem did ^Ehappy mek dem a ^Ecelebrate.

_____

9. ^EClean shi did a ^Eclean aar ^Eshoes wid di ^Eshoe ^Epolish.

_____

10. Sen mi ^Euncle aggo sen wi ^Emoney.

_____

Practice Exercise 21

Rewrite the following sentences to the passive voice of English.

1. Kamisha placed the phone on the table.

_____

2. The rubbish disposal company picked up the rubbish.

_____

3. The father picked up the baby from the crib.

_____

4. The girl hangs her sweater in the closet.

_____

5. He kicked the ball over the fence.

_____

6. Kenya made her bed early this morning.

   _____

7. We packed our bags five days before our trip.

   _____

8. The children are playing with the dog in the yard.

   _____

9. The television is playing loudly in the living room.

   _____

10. They flew to Haiti before flying home to Jamaica.

   _____

Practice Exercise 22

Translate the sentences that you completed in Practice Exercise 21 to Jamaican Creole.

1. _____
2. _____
3. _____
4. _____
5. _____
6. _____
7. _____
8. _____
9. _____
10. _____

Practice Exercise 23

Identify whether the following Jamaican Creole sentences are in the active voice or passive voice by writing *active voice* or *passive voice* on the line.

1. Mi goh a di shuo ᴱtwo ᴱtime areddi.

   _____

2. A yessideh im did ᴱplan fi ᴱcomplete im huomwok.

   _____

3. ᴱKick im did a ᴱkick di ᴱball ᴱwhen im jap.

   _____

4. A did ᴱone touz'n dalla mi pyeh fi di ᴱshirt.

   _____

5. ᴱSammy ᴱput im unifaam pan di ᴱline fi ᴱdry.

   _____

6. Di puosman diliva di myel pan ᴱtime.

   _____

7. ᴶDi ᴶshuo get cancel by ᴶdi movie company.

   _____

8. ᴱErrol ᴱtravel fi ᴱtwo owa goh a wok evridyeh.

   _____

9. Di bwuay nuo ᴱhow fi jaiv di kyaar.

   _____

10. Di ᴱmusic tiicha aggo ᴱallow ᴱone muo ᴱstudent fi ᴱjoin di ban.

    _____

Practice Exercise 24

Translate the sentences that you completed in Practice Exercise 23 to English.

1. _____
2. _____
3. _____
4. _____
5. _____
6. _____
7. _____
8. _____
9. _____
10. _____

Practice Exercise 25

Use the following words to form sentences in the passive voice of Jamaican Creole. Identify the part of speech of the word you used by writing it on the line (e.g. noun, verb, etc.).

aada *n., v.* order   **eniweh** *adv., pron.* anywhere
ajos *v.* adjust   **faak** *n., v.* fork
bifuo *adv., conj., prep.* before   **gaaliin** *n.* egret
doppi *n.* ghost

1. _____

    Part of speech _____
2. _____

    Part of speech _____
3. _____

    Part of speech _____
4. _____

Part of speech _____

5. _____

Part of speech _____

6. _____

Part of speech _____

7. _____

Part of speech _____

Making a Sentence Negative

To make a sentence negative in English, auxiliary and modal auxiliary verbs are used in combination with *not*. An auxiliary verb acts as a helping verb to the main verb. The auxiliary verbs of English include *do*, *have*, and *be*. Examples of negative sentences in English include:

He does not expect it.

We have not taken the bus to school.

They are not from here.

Kenroy is not at home.

Negative Auxiliary Verbs of Jamaican Creole

In Jamaican Creole, the negative auxiliary verb used depends on the tense of the sentence. Note that *not* is pronounced as it is in English. The negative auxiliary verbs used in Jamaican Creole are listed below.

Auxiliary Verbs	Also Used As	Used In
noh		present tense
dooh		present tense
duo		present tense
naah		present continuous tense
not iiv'n	niiv'n, neev'n, noh iiv'n	present tense, present perfect tense, past tense

Auxiliary Verbs	Also Used As	Used In
not iiv'n did	niiv'n did, neev'n did, noh iiv'n did, not iiv'n beeh, not iiv'n weeh, niiv'n beeh, niiv'n weeh, neev'n beeh, neev'n weeh, noh iiv'n beeh, noh iiv'n weeh	past tense, past perfect tense
neva	nebba, neeh	present perfect tense, past tense
neva did	nebba did, neeh did	past tense, past perfect tense

Noh, Dooh, and Duo

Noh, *dooh*, and *duo* are used in the present tense. *Noh* means *not*, *does not*, *do not*, *has not*, and *have not*. It is used with the base infinitive form of the verb. *Dooh* and *duo* mean *does not*, *do not*, *has not*, and *have not*. They are also used with the base infinitive form of the verb but are used less frequently than *noh*. For example:

Jamaican Creole	English
Jillian noh fain ih inna di room.	Jillian has not found it in the room.
Wi duo ha enough food fi di paati.	We do not have enough food for the party.
Shi dooh siit.	She does not see it.

The Verb Bi When Used with Noh

The verb *bi* is formed *a* when used with *noh*. Together, *a* and *noh* mean *am not*, *is not*, and *are not*. For example:

Jamaican Creole	English
Im a noh paat a wi group.	He is not part of our group.
Simone an Sheena a noh fren.	Simone and Sheena are not friends.
Mi a noh wau good daansa.	I am not a good dancer.

When Bi and Noh Are Used with Adjectives

Whenever the verb *bi* occurs with *noh* before an adjective, the verb is omitted and only *noh* is used. For example:

Jamaican Creole	English
Kerona <u>noh</u> happy.	lit. Kerona <u>not</u> happy.
	(Kerona is not happy.)
Di byebi <u>noh</u> well.	lit. The baby <u>not</u> well.
	(The baby is not well.)
Dem kyaar <u>noh</u> new.	lit. Their car <u>not</u> new.
	(Their car is not new.)

When Bi and Noh Are Used with Prepositions and Adverbs

When used before prepositions such as *a, pau, pan, inna, oova, anda*, etc., and adverbs such as *ya, deh, dyer*, etc., that refer to the location or position of the subject, the verb becomes *deh*. For example:

Jamaican Creole	English
Monica <u>noh deh</u> deh.	Monica <u>is not</u> there.
Ih <u>noh deh</u> anda di tyeb'l.	It <u>is not</u> under the table.
Dem <u>noh deh</u> inna di maakit.	They <u>are not</u> in the market.

Jamaicans sometimes omit the verb before *inna, oova, anda*, and *dong*. An example of this is *Shi noh inna di office* (E. *She is not in the office*).

Naah

Naah is used in the present continuous tense. *Naah* is used to indicate what is currently not taking place. It means *is not* or *are not*. For example:

Jamaican Creole	English
Wi <u>naah goh</u> a di shuo.	We <u>are not going</u> to the show.
Im <u>naah tell</u> di chruut.	He <u>is not telling</u> the truth.
Nelly <u>naah goh</u> pan di trip.	Nelly <u>is not going</u> on the trip.

The Verb Bi and Naah

The verb *bi* is used in its base infinitve form (*bi*) when used with *naah*. For example:

Jamaican Creole	English
Shi <u>naah bi</u> fyer.	She <u>is not being</u> fair.
Lionel <u>naah bi</u> im bes man.	Lionel <u>is not being</u> his best man.
Im <u>naah bi</u> haness.	He <u>is not being</u> honest.

Not liv'n

Not iiv'n (sometimes used as *niiv'n, neev'n,* or *noh iiv'n*) is used in the present tense, the present perfect tense, and the past tense. *Not iiv'n* means *does not even, do not even, has not even, have not even,* and *did not even.* For example:

Jamaican Creole	English
Dem <u>not iiv'n clean</u> di house.	They <u>have not even cleaned</u> the house.
Di pikni <u>niiv'n nuo</u> di uhman.	The child <u>does not even know</u> the woman.
Shakina <u>neev'n iht</u> breakfast, an shi gone a wok.	Shakina <u>did not even eat</u> breakfast, and she has gone to work.

Note that *noh iiv'n* is not frequently used to mean *did not even.*

The Verb Bi When Used with Not liv'n, Niiv'n, Neev'n, or Noh iiv'n

When the verb *bi* is used with *not iiv'n* (also used as *niiv'n, neev'n,* or *noh iiv'n*), it is conjugated *a.* Together, they mean *am not even, is not even,* and *are not even.* Note that the verb *a* can come before or after *not iiv'n, niiv'n, neev'n,* and *noh iiv'n.* For example:

Jamaican Creole	English
Yanique <u>not iiv'n a</u> mi fren.	lit. Yanique <u>not even is</u> my friend.
	(*Yanique is not even my friend.*)
Omar <u>a neev'n</u> ten yet.	Omar <u>is not even</u> ten yet.
<u>A niiv'n</u> di right ansa.	It <u>is not even</u> the right answer.

When Bi and Not Iiv'n, Niiv'n, Neev'n, or Noh Iiv'n Are Used with Prepositions and Adverbs

When used before prepositions such as *a, pau, pan, inna, oova, anda,* etc., and adverbs such as *ya, deh, dyer,* etc., that state the location or position of the subject, the verb is formed *deh.* For example:

Jamaican Creole	English
Deeh <u>niiv'n deh</u> deh yet.	They <u>are not even</u> there yet.
Kerron <u>noh iiv'n deh</u> inna im classroom.	Kerron <u>is not even</u> in his classroom.
Di daag <u>neev'n deh</u> inna di yaad.	The dog <u>is not even</u> in the yard.

Speakers of Jamaican Creole sometimes omit the verb before *inna, oova, anda,* and *dong.* An example is *Di cat niiv'n inna di box* (E. *The cat is not even in the box*).

When Bi and Not Iiv'n, Niiv'n, Neev'n, or Noh Iiv'n Are Used with Adjectives

When the verb *bi* occurs with *not iiv'n, niiv'n, neev'n,* or *noh iiv'n* before an adjective, the verb is omitted and only *not iiv'n, niiv'n, neev'n,* or *noh iiv'n* is used. For example:

Jamaican Creole	English
Jerome <u>not iiv'n</u> sick.	lit. Jerome <u>not even</u> sick.
	(*Jerome is not even sick.*)
Deeh <u>neev'n</u> upset bout ih.	lit. They <u>not even</u> upset about it.
	(*They are not even upset about it.*)
Di house <u>niiv'n</u> clean.	lit. The house <u>not even</u> clean.
	(*The house is not even clean.*)

Not liv'n Did

Not iiv'n did (sometimes used as *niiv'n did, neev'n did,* or *noh iiv'n did*) is used in the past and past perfect tense. It means *did not even* and *had not even.* Jamaicans sometimes use *beeh* or *weeh* in place of *did.*

In these cases the auxiliary verb would become:

not iiv'n beeh	not iiv'n weeh
niiv'n beeh	niiv'n weeh
neev'n beeh	neev'n weeh
noh iiv'n beeh	noh iiv'n weeh

Here are some examples of the verb *bi* with *not iiv'n did,* etc.:

Jamaican Creole	English
Wi <u>neev'n beeh expek</u> fi siim.	We <u>did not even expect</u> to see him.
Di donkey <u>not iiv'n did iht</u> di grass.	The donkey <u>had not even eaten</u> the grass.
Di uhman <u>noh iiv'n weeh plan</u> fi di staam.	The woman <u>had not even planned</u> for the storm.

The Verb Bi When Used with Not liv'n Did, Niiv'n Did, Neev'n Did, or Noh liv'n Did

When the verb *bi* is used with *not iiv'n did, niiv'n did, neev'n did,* or *noh iiv'n did,* it is formed *a.* Together they mean *was not even, were not even,* and *had not even been.* Jamaicans sometimes use *ben a* or *wen a* in place of *did a.* In these cases the auxiliary verb would become:

not iiv'n ben a	not iiv'n wen a
niiv'n ben a	niiv'n wen a
neev'n ben a	neev'n wen a
noh iiv'n ben a	noh iiv'n wen a

Note that when the subject of the verb is *ih* (E. *it*), *a* comes before *not iiv'n did, niiv'n did, neev'n did,* and *noh iiv'n did.*

Here are some examples of the verb *bi* with *not iiv'n did,* etc.:

Jamaican Creole	English
A noh iiv'n did di syem blouse.	It was not even the same blouse.
Sheldon neev'n wen a aar fren.	Sheldon was not even her friend.
Im not iiv'n did a di liida a di group.	He had not even been the leader of the group.

When Bi and Not Iiv'n Did, Niiv'n Did, Neev'n Did, or Noh Iiv'n Did Are Used Before Prepositions and Adverbs

When used before prepositions such as as *a, pau, pan, inna, oova, anda,* etc., and adverbs such as *ya, deh, dyer,* etc., that state the location or position of the subject, the verb becomes *deh.* For example:

Jamaican Creole	English
Deeh niiv'n weeh deh pan time.	They had not even been on time.
Jerome an im bredda neev'n did deh huom.	Jerome and his brother had not even been home.
Di dacta noh iiv'n beeh deh inna im office.	The doctor had not even been in his office.

Jamaicans sometimes omit the verb before *inna, oova, anda,* and *dong.* An example is *Di envelope not iiv'n did inna di bag* (E. *The envelope had not even been in the bag*).

When Bi and Not Iiv'n Did, Niiv'n Did, Neev'n Did, or Noh Iiv'n Did Are Used Before Adjectives

When the verb *bi* is used with an adjective to refer to the state of the subject, the verb is omitted and only *not iiv'n did* (*not iiv'n beeh, not iiv'n weeh, niiv'n did, niiv'n beeh, niiv'n weeh, neev'n did, neev'n beeh, neev'n weeh, noh iiv'n did, noh iiv'n beeh,* or *noh iiv'n weeh*) is used. For example:

Jamaican Creole	English
Im niiv'n did iiga fi goh.	He was not even eager to go.
Di mango neev'n beeh ripe.	The mango had not even been ripe.
Di banana not iiv'n weeh yellow.	The banana was not even yellow.

Neva

Neva (sometimes used as *nebba* or *neeh*) is used in the present perfect and past tense. It means *did not, has never,* and *have never.* For example:

Jamaican Creole	English
Wi <u>nebba si</u> dem, eva.	We <u>have never seen</u> them, ever.
Karen <u>neva wok</u> a night, yet.	Karen <u>has never worked</u> at night, ever.
Iih <u>neeh iht</u>.	He <u>did not eat</u>.

The Verb Bi When Used with Neva, Nebba, Or Neeh

When the verb *bi* is used with *neva, nebba,* or *neeh,* it is conjugated *a.* Together they mean *was not, were not, was never,* and *were never.* Note that the verb *a* can be placed before or after *neva, nebba,* and *neeh.* When used with *ih* or E. *it, a* is always placed before *neva, nebba,* and *neeh.*

Here are some examples of the use of *neva, nebba,* and *neeh:*

Jamaican Creole	English
<u>A neeh</u> da one deh.	It <u>was not</u> that one.
Nikiesha <u>neva a</u> wau priifek.	Nikiesha <u>was never</u> a prefect.
Di bwuay <u>a neeh</u> di ong'l one weh did deh deh.	The boy <u>was not</u> the only one that was there.

When Bi is Used with Neva, Nebba, or Neeh
Before Prepositions and Adverbs

When used before prepositions such as *a, pau, pan, inna, oova, anda,* etc., and adverbs such as *ya, deh, dyer,* etc., that state the location or position of the subject, the verb is formed *deh.* When used with *deh,* the auxiliary verbs *neva, nebba,* and *neeh* can also mean *is never* and *are never,* especially if an adverb is used to give an estimation of time.

Here are some examples:

Jamaican Creole	English
Deeh <u>neva deh</u> ya, eva.	They <u>are never</u> here, ever.
Pam <u>neeh deh</u> inna di room.	Pam <u>was not</u> in the room.
Mi sista <u>nebba deh</u> a di concert.	My sister <u>was not</u> at the concert.

Speakers of Jamaican Creole sometimes omit the verb before *inna*, *oova*, *anda*, and *dong*. An example is *Tom neva oova dyer* (E. *Tom was not over there*).

When Bi is Used with Neva, Nebba, or Neeh Before Adjectives

When the verb *bi* occurs with *neva*, *neeh*, or *nebba* before an adjective, the verb is omitted and only *neva*, *nebba*, or *neeh* is used. When used with an adjective, *neva*, *nebba*, and *neeh* can also mean *is never* and *are never*, especially if an adverb is used to give an estimation of time.

Here are some examples:

Jamaican Creole	English
Di house dem <u>neva</u> dotti.	The houses <u>are never</u> dirty.
Di juok <u>neeh</u> funny.	The joke <u>was not</u> funny.
Shi <u>nebba</u> untidy, eva.	She <u>is never</u> untidy, ever.

Neva Did, Nebba Did, or Neeh Did

Neva did (sometimes used as *nebba did* or *neeh did*) is used in the past tense and past perfect tense. It means *did not*, *had not*, and *had never*. Jamaicans sometimes use *beeh* or *weeh* in place of *did*. In this case, the verb phrase becomes:

neva beeh	neva weeh
nebba beeh	nebba weeh
neeh beeh	neeh weeh

They also use *beeh* or *weeh* together with *did*. The verb phrase becomes:

neva beeh did	neva weeh did
nebba beeh did	nebba weeh did
neeh beeh did	neeh weeh did

Here are some examples of the verb *bi* with *neva did*, etc.:

Jamaican Creole	**English**
Iih <u>neva weeh did siit</u> bifuo inna im life.	He <u>had never seen</u> it before in his life.
Patsy <u>neeh did wok</u> laas week.	Patsy <u>did not work</u> last week.
Im <u>nebba beeh duh</u> it.	He <u>had not done</u> it.

The Verb Bi When Used with Neva Did, Nebba Did, or Neeh Did

When the verb *bi* is used with *neva did* (also used as *nebba did* or *neeh did*), it is formed *a*. Together, *neva did*, *nebba did*, or *neeh did* and *a* mean *was not, were not, was never, were never, had not been*, and *had never been*. Note that *a* comes after *neva did, nebba did*, and *neeh did* in the sentence except when the verb is used after *ih* (E. *it*).

Jamaicans sometimes use *beeh* or *weeh* in place of *did*. In this case, the verb phrase is used as:

neva beeh	neva weeh
nebba beeh	nebba weeh
neeh beeh	neeh weeh

Jamaicans also use *beeh* or *weeh* together with *did*. The verb phrase in this case is used as:

neva beeh did	neva weeh did
nebba beeh did	nebba weeh did
neeh beeh did	neeh weeh did

Here are some examples of the verb *bi* when used with *neva did*, *nebba*, etc.:

Jamaican Creole	English
Judy <u>neva weeh did a</u> mi employee.	Judy <u>was never</u> my employee.
<u>A neeh did</u> da one deh.	It <u>was not</u> that one.
Di ban <u>neva did a</u> di bes back den.	The band <u>had not been</u> the best back then.

When Bi is Used with Neva Did, Nebba Did, or Neeh Did Before Prepositions and Adverbs

When used before prepositions such as *a, pau, pan, inna, oova, anda*, etc., and adverbs such as *ya, deh, dyer*, etc., that state the location or position of the subject, the verb becomes *deh*. For example:

Jamaican Creole	English
Suzette an Davina <u>neva did deh</u> huom.	Suzette and Davina <u>had not been</u> home.
Pam <u>neeh did deh</u> inna di building.	Pam <u>had not been</u> in the building.
Mi bredda <u>neeh beeh did deh</u> a di gyem.	My brother <u>had not been</u> at the game.

Speakers of Jamaican Creole sometimes omit the verb before *inna, oova, anda*, and *dong*. An example is *Di envelope neva did inna di bag* (E. *The envelope had not been in the bag*).

When Bi is Used with Neva Did, Nebba Did, or Neeh Did Before Adjectives

When the verb *bi* is used with an adjective to indicate the state of the subject, the verb is omitted and only *neva did, nebba did*, or *neeh did, etc.* is used. For example:

Jamaican Creole	English
Im <u>neva beeh</u> happy.	He [was] <u>not</u> happy.
Dem <u>neeh weeh did</u> frenli.	They [were] <u>not</u> friendly.

Jamaican Creole	English
Dina <u>neva did</u> busy.	lit. Dina <u>had not</u> busy.
	(Dina had not been busy.)

Practice Exercise 26

Translate the following sentences to Jamaican Creole.

1. Garret and Hadley are not staying for more than three days.

   _____

2. We have not done the work that is necessary to finish the project on time.

   _____

3. I am not old enough to take public transportation alone.

   _____

4. They have not even spoken about the issue.

   _____

5. Mary has never been to the city.

   _____

6. The bus does not go to the rural parts of the country.

   _____

7. That man is not his grandfather.

   _____

8. She has not left the classroom yet.

   _____

9. The students have never gone rafting on the Rio Grande.

   _____

10. It is never hot and humid in winter.

    _____

Practice Exercise 27

Use the following list of auxiliary verbs to form Jamaican Creole sentences of your own.

neva did	niiv'n	naah	noh	duo
not iiv'n did	neev'n	neeh	nebba did	nebba

1. _____
2. _____
3. _____
4. _____
5. _____
6. _____
7. _____
8. _____
9. _____
10. _____

Practice Exercise 28

Translate the Jamaican Creole Sentences from Practice Exercise 27 to English.

1. _____
2. _____
3. _____
4. _____
5. _____
6. _____
7. _____
8. _____

9. _____

10. _____

Practice Exercise 29

Underline the negative auxiliary verbs in the following sentences, and then rewrite the sentences in English.

1. ᴶDi cleaning company ᴶnaah come clean ᴶdi store ᴶtudeh.

   _____

2. Shi niiv'n ᴱtell wi seh shi neeh did tek di ᴱmoney ᴱout a di ᴱaccount.

   _____

3. ᴱDamion duo nuo weh im bredda an im coz'n deh.

   _____

4. A neva soh im did seh yessideh.

   _____

5. Mi noh tink mi aggo deh deh, an im noh wau fi goh ᴱby imself.

   _____

6. Di ᴱemployee dem ᴱbelieve seh di ᴱnew manija noh ᴱgood pan di wok.

   _____

7. Mi nebba si noh'n lakka dat inna mi ᴱlife.

   _____

8. ᶠFrank faada noh expeck im fi fyel im tes.

   _____

9. ᴱKimone neva did deh a ᴱschool ᴱwhen di tiicha ᴱteach di ᴱtopic, soh shi noh andastan ᴱhow fi duh di ᴱassignment.

   _____

10. ᴱMona dooh ᴱwash di ᴱdishes dem weh aar madda seh shi fi ᴱwash.

Practice Exercise 30

Translate the Jamaican Creole Sentences from Practice Exercise 29 to English.

1. _____

2. _____

3. _____

4. _____

5. _____

6. _____

7. _____

8. _____

9. _____

10. _____

Practice Exercise 31

Use the following words and any of the negative auxiliary verbs previously discussed to form negative sentences in Jamaican Creole. Identify the part of speech of the word you used by writing it on the line (e.g. noun, verb, etc.).

aan *adv.* on

barro *v.* borrow

grong *n.* field; farm; ground

piini/piini walli *n.* firefly

red-yai *adj., n.* envious; envy

sih'n *adv., pron., n.* thing; something

taiyad *adj., v.* tired; tire

MAKING A SENTENCE NEGATIVE

1. _____

   Part of speech _____

2. _____

   Part of speech _____

3. _____

   Part of speech _____

4. _____

   Part of speech _____

5. _____

   Part of speech _____

6. _____

   Part of speech _____

7. _____

   Part of speech _____

The Negative Modal Auxiliary Verbs

The modal auxiliary verb is a type of auxiliary verb. It cannot be conjugated and has no participles. Modal auxiliary verbs are sometimes used before auxiliary verbs in a verb phrase. An example is *should have known*, where *should* is the modal auxiliary verb. *Not* is added to the verb phrase in order to make it negative.

The modal auxiliary verbs of English are:

can	ought to
could	shall
may	should
might	will
must	would

For example:

The mechanic said he could not fix the bike, so he will return the money.

In Jamaican Creole, the negative modal auxiliary verbs are:

wi noh (or noh wi)	cud'na
*might noh	wud'n
noh fi (or noffi)	shud'n
naah goh	kyaah
mos'n	cud'n
wud'na	

Might is pronounced as in English.

74

Some modal auxiliary verbs used in Jamaican Creole require *noh* to form their negative. These include *wi*, *might*, and *fi*.

Wi Noh

In the conditional future tense of Jamaican Creole, *wi* (E. *will*) is used along with an *if* or *when* clause. *Wi noh* (sometimes used as *noh wi*) means *will not* and is the negative version of *wi*. For example:

Jamaican Creole	English
Fitzroy <u>wi noh</u> agree wid yuh.	Fitzroy <u>will (possibly/might) not</u> agree with you.
Dem <u>wi noh</u> badda come.	They <u>will (possibly/might) not</u> bother [to] come.
Iiv'n if Sherry ha wau tes tomorrow, shi <u>noh wi</u> badda fi study.	Even if Sherry has a test tomorrow, she <u>will (possibly/might) not</u> bother to study.

Wi Noh and the Verb Bi

The verb *bi* is used with *wi noh* as it is with the modal auxiliary *wi*. It is used in its base infinitive form *bi*. *Wi noh bi* means *will (possibly/ might) not be*. It can also be used as *noh wi bi*.

E.g., *Dem wi noh bi happy if yuh leave* (E. *They will [possibly] not be happy if you leave*).

The verb *bi* is sometimes omitted before adjectives in Jamaican Creole:

E.g., *Dem noh wi aarait* (E. *They will [possibly/might not] be alright*).

In Jamaican Creole, the verb *bi* becomes *deh* when used directly before prepositions such as *a*, *pau*, *pan*, *inna*, *oova*, *anda*, etc., and adverbs such as *ya*, *deh*, *dyer*, etc., that state the position or location of the subject.

E.g., *Shi wi noh deh deh when yuh goh deh* (E. *She will [possibly] not be there when you go there*).

The verb *bi* is sometimes omitted before *inna, oova, anda, dong, agens, afta,* and *aaf.*

E.g., *Di daag wi noh inna di yaad* (E. *The dog will (possibly) not be in the yard*).

The verb is never omitted before *a, pan, pau, dyer,* and *ya* in Jamaican Creole.

Might Noh

Might noh is used in Jamaican Creole as *might not* is used in English. For example:

Jamaican Creole	English
Jabary win di prize, but iih family dem <u>might noh</u> nuo.	Jabary won the prize, but his family <u>might not</u> know.
Shi <u>might noh</u> wau di book dem fi deh dehsoh.	She <u>might not</u> want the books to be right there.
Di apple <u>might noh</u> ripe.	The apple <u>might not</u> be ripe.

Might Noh and the Verb Bi

The verb *bi* is used in its base infinitive form after *might noh*. *Might noh bi* means *might not be.*

E.g., *Dem might noh bi early* (E. *They might not be early*).

The verb *bi* is usually omitted before adjectives in Jamaican Creole.

E.g., *Shi might noh happy wid yuh decision* (E. *She might not be happy with your decision*).

In Jamaican Creole, the verb *bi* becomes *deh* when used directly before prepositions such as *a, pau, pan, inna, oova, anda,* etc., and adverbs such as *ya, deh, dyer,* etc., that state the position or location of the subject.

E.g., *Letisha might noh deh a class* (E. *Letisha might not be at class*).

The verb *bi* is sometimes omitted before *inna, oova, anda, dong, agens, afta,* and *aaf.*

E.g., *Di book might noh inna di bag* (E. *The book might not be in the bag*).

The verb is never omitted before *a, pan, pau, deh, dyer,* and *ya.*

Noh Fi

Noh fi (*noffi*) means *ought not to* or *should not.* The following are examples of its use:

Jamaican Creole	English
Dem <u>noffi</u> duh dat.	They <u>ought not to</u> do that.
Mi <u>noffi</u> iht nof shuga.	I <u>should not</u> eat a lot of sugar.
Shemar <u>noffi</u> gi dem di money.	Shemar <u>should not</u> give them the money.

Noh Fi and the Verb Bi

The verb *bi* is used in its base infinitive form after *noh fi.*

E.g., *People noh fi bi silent bout di problem* (E. *People should not be silent about the problem.*

The verb *bi* is sometimes omitted before adjectives.

E.g., *Wi noh fi sad bout ih* (E. *We should not be sad about it*).

The verb becomes *deh* when used directly before prepositions such as *a, pau, pan, inna, oova, anda,* etc., and adverbs such as *ya, deh, dyer,* etc., that state the position or location of the subject.

E.g., *Di pikini dem noh fi deh inna Maas Joe grong* (E. *The children should not be in Mr. Joe's field*).

The verb is sometimes omitted before *inna, oova, anda, dong, agens, afta,* and *aaf.*

E.g., *Wi noh fi inna di store during school time* (E. *We should not be in the store during school time*).

The verb is never omitted before *a, pan, pau, deh, dyer,* and *ya.*

Naah Goh

Naah goh (sometimes abbreviated *naah*) means *is not going to, are not going to,* and *will not*. For example:

Jamaican Creole	English
Alana <u>naah goh rimemba</u> fi tek out di gyabij.	Alana <u>will not remember</u> to take out the garbage.
Wi <u>naah si</u> dem tomorrow.	We <u>will not see</u> them tomorrow.
Petrina dem <u>naah goh allow</u> yuh fi goh wid dem.	Petrina [and the others] <u>are not going to allow</u> you to go with them.

Naah Goh and the Verb Bi

The verb *bi* is used in its base infinitive form after *naah goh*.

E.g., *Amoy naah goh bi aar bridesmaid* (E. *Amoy will not be her bridesmaid*).

The verb *bi* is sometimes omitted before adjectives.

E.g., *Jenny naah goh upset seh Amoy naah goh bi aar bridesmaid* (E. *Jenny will not be upset that Amoy will not be her bridesmaid*).

The verb becomes *deh* when used directly before prepositions such as *a, pau, pan, inna, oova, anda,* etc., and adverbs such as *ya, deh, dyer,* etc., that state the position or location of the subject.

E.g., *Dem naah goh deh a di wedding* (E. *They will not be at the wedding*).

The verb is sometimes omitted before *inna, oova, anda, dong, agens, afta,* and *aaf.*

E.g., *Wi naah goh inna di hotel* (E. *We will not be in the hotel*).

The verb is never omitted before *a, pan, pau, deh, dyer,* and *ya.*

Wud'na

Wud'na (sometimes used as *wud'na beeh, wud'na did, wud'na weeh, wud'n beeh, wud'n did,* or *wud'n weeh*) is used with the present perfect tense. It means *would not have*. It is used in Jamaican Creole as *would not have* is used in English. For example:

Jamaican Creole	English
Di people dem <u>wud'na beeh</u> gyadda inna di square pau wau Monday.	The people <u>would not have</u> gathered in the square on a Monday.
Linval <u>wud'na did</u> siit if yuh neva did tell im.	Linval <u>would not have</u> seen it if you had not told him.
Di girl <u>wud'na</u> gi dem.	The girl <u>would not have</u> given [it to] them.

Wud'na and the Verb Bi

Wud'na (also used as *wud'na beeh, wud'na did, wud'na weeh, wud'n beeh, wud'n did,* or *wud'n weeh*) is used with the verb *bi* to mean *would not have been*. The verb *bi* is generally used in its base infinitive form.

E.g., *Kiran wud'na bi soh taiyad if im neva wok* (E. *Kiran would not have been so tired if he did not work*).

The verb becomes *deh* when used directly before prepositions such as *a, pau, pan, inna, oova, anda,* etc., and adverbs such as *ya, deh, dyer,* etc., that state the position or location of the subject.

E.g., *Tisha wud'na deh a St. Mary if shi did busy* (*Tisha would not have been in St. Mary if she were busy*).

The verb is sometimes omitted before adjectives, and *wud'na* is sometimes abbreviated *wud'n* before them.

E.g., *Di man wud'n upset if dem did tell im* (*The man would not be upset if they had told him*).

The verb is sometimes omitted before *inna, oova, anda, dong, agens, afta,* and *aaf. Wud'na* is sometimes abbreviated *wud'n* before these prepositions.

E.g., *Darren wud'n inna di store* (E. *Darren would not be in the store*).

The verb is never omitted before *a, pan, pau, deh, dyer,* and *ya.*

Cud'na

Cud'na (sometimes used as *cud'na beeh, cud'na did, cud'na weeh, cud'n beeh, cud'n did,* or *cud'n weeh*) is used in the present perfect tense. It means *could not have*. It is used in Jamaican Creole as *could not have* is used in English. For example:

Jamaican Creole	English
Im <u>cud'n did</u> si roun di ben.	He <u>could not have</u> seen around the bend/corner.
Shiona <u>cud'na beeh</u> nuo dat.	Shiona <u>could not have</u> known that.
Mi faada <u>cud'na</u> lef lyeta.	My father <u>could not have</u> left later.

Cud'na and the Verb Bi

Cud'na is used with the verb *bi* to mean *could not have been*. The verb is generally used in its base infinitive form with *cud'na.*

E.g., *Ih cud'na bi mi* (E. *It could not have been me*).

The verb becomes *deh* when used directly before prepositions such as *a, pau, pan, inna, oova, anda,* etc., and adverbs such as *ya, deh, dyer,* etc., that state the position or location of the subject.

E.g., *Shi cud'na deh a wi graduation* (E. *She could not have been at our graduation*).

The verb is sometimes omitted before adjectives.

E.g., *Mi faada cud'na angry wid wi* (E. *My father could not have been angry with us*).

The verb is sometimes omitted before *inna, oova, anda, dong, agens, afta,* and *aaf. Cud'na* is sometimes abbreviated *cud'n* before these prepositions.

E.g., *Mi cud'na inna di group if a neva fi him* (E. *I could not have been in the group if it weren't for him*).

The verb is never omitted before *a, pan, pau, deh, dyer,* and *ya.*

Other Modal Auxiliary Verbs

The remaining modal auxiliary verbs of Jamaican Creole and English are:

Jamaican Creole	English
wud'n	would not
shud'n	should not
cud'n	could not
mos'n	must not
kyaah	cannot

They are used in Jamaican Creole as they are used in English. For example:

Jamaican Creole	English
Kerry cud'n tell im.	Kerry could not tell him.
Mi shud'n goh deh.	I should not go there.
Shi wud'n sign di pyepa dem.	She would not sign the papers.

The Verb Bi and the Remaining Modal Auxiliary Verbs

The verb *bi* is used in its base infinitive form after *wud'n, shud'n, cud'n, mos'n,* and *kyaah.*

E.g., *Mi wud'n bi happy deh* (E. *I would not be happy there*).

The verb is sometimes omitted before adjectives.

E.g., *Yuh mos'n sad bout ih* (E. *You must not be sad about it*).

The verb becomes *deh* when used directly before prepositions such as *a, pau, pan, inna, oova, anda,* etc., and adverbs such as *ya, deh, dyer,* etc., that state the position or location of the subject.

E.g., *Mi cud'n deh a di shuo laas night* (E. *I could not be at the show last night*).

The verb is sometimes omitted before *inna, oova, anda, dong, agens, afta,* and *aaf.*

E.g. *Di ring kyaah anda di couch* (E. *The ring cannot be under the couch*).

The verb is never omitted before *a, pan, pau, deh, dyer,* and *ya.*

The Negative Passive Voice

The negative passive voice of Jamaican Creole is formed by using the following verb phrases at the beginning of the sentence:

Verb Phrase	Also Used As	Meaning
a noh		it is not
a neva	a nebba or a neeh	it was not
a noh did	noh beeh or a noh weeh	it was not
a neva did	a nebba beeh, a nebba did, a nebba weeh, a neeh beeh, a neeh did, or a neeh weeh	it was not

Examples of the use of *a noh*:

Jamaican Creole	English
A noh soh im seh.	lit. It is not so he said. *(That is not what he said.)*
A noh true weh dem seh.	It is not true what they say.
A noh shi dem a look fa.	It is not she [who] they are looking for.

Examples of the use of *a neva*, *a noh did*, and *a neva did*:

Jamaican Creole	English
<u>A neva did</u> Dwayne im tell.	<u>It was not</u> Dwayne [whom] he told.
<u>A nebba weeh</u> him did seh soh.	<u>It was not</u> he [who] said so.
<u>A noh did</u> soh ih goh.	lit. <u>It was not</u> how it went.
	(*That was not how it was.*)

The Double Negative Structure of Jamaican Creole

The double negative structure is grammatically incorrect in English. For example, the sentence *I don't know nothing* would be considered incorrect in English because both *don't* and *nothing* are negative words. The sentence would be correctly written as *I don't know anything* or *I know nothing*.

The double negative structure is, however, acceptable in Jamaican Creole and is most frequently used. It is common to replace positive adjectives, adverbs, and pronouns with negative ones to make the sentence negative. Some of the common ones are listed below.

Negative Words Used To Replace Common Adjectives, Adverbs, And Pronouns

	Replaced In Jamaican Creole By:		
	Adjective	*Adverb*	*Pronoun*
any (*adj., adv., pron.*)	[E] no	[E] no	[E] none
anybody (*pron.*)	n/a	n/a	[E] nobody
anymore (*adv.*)	n/a	noomuo/nomo	n/a
anywhere (*adv., pron.*)	n/a	nooweh/noweh	noowch/noweh
somebody (*pron.*)	n/a	n/a	[E] nobody
something (*adv., pron.*)	n/a	noh'n/noting	noh'n/noting
somewhere (*adv., pron.*)	n/a	noowch/noweh	n/a

When the Verb Takes a Negative

In English, the sentence can be structured so that the verb takes the negative and not the object (e.g., *We will not go anywhere*). In Jamaican Creole, both the verb and the object take a negative form. For example:

Jamaican Creole	English
Mi <u>noh duh noh'n</u> frau maanin.	lit. I <u>did not do nothing</u> from morning.
	(*I have not done anything since morning.*)
Nelisha <u>noh wau nomo</u>.	lit. Nelisha <u>does not want no more</u>.
	(*Nelisha does not want any more.*)
Di pikini dem <u>naah goh nooweh</u>.	lit. The children <u>are not going nowhere</u>.
	(*The children are not going anywhere.*)

When the Object Takes a Negative

Likewise, the sentence can be structured so that the object takes the negative in English (e.g., *Rita has no money*). Both the verb and the object take a negative in Jamaican Creole. For example:

Jamaican Creole	English
Di store <u>noh ha no waata</u>.	lit. The store <u>does not have no water</u>.
	(*The store has no water.*)
<u>Nobody neva did a celebrate</u> tudeh.	lit. <u>Nobody had not been celebrating</u> today.
	(*Nobody had been celebrating today.*)
<u>No flowa noh deh</u> inna di cupboard.	lit. <u>No flour is not</u> in the cupboard.
	(*No flour is in the cupboard.*)

Practice Exercise 32

Translate the following negative sentences to Jamaican Creole.

1. Anita cannot play the piano, but she can play the flute.

    _____

2. I might not be able to attend the graduation next week.

    _____

3. Ken could not pay back the money because he had not worked
    for over a month.

    _____

4. If they had known that she would not be there, they would not
    have gone.

    _____

5. Children should not forget to study, or they will be behind in
    their lessons.

    _____

6. Lina will not tell us what happened.

    _____

7. The man would not take the money because it was not his.

    _____

8. The store might not be open when we get there.

    _____

9. Roy should not travel so late at night.

    _____

10. The children ought not to climb over the fence because it is
    private property.

    _____

Practice Exercise 33

Translate the sentences that you completed in Practice Exercise 32 to English.

1. _____
2. _____
3. _____
4. _____
5. _____
6. _____
7. _____
8. _____
9. _____
10. _____

Practice Exercise 34

Use the following list of modal auxiliary verbs to form Jamaican Creole sentences of your own.

| wi noh | noh fi | wud'n | cud'na | shud'n |
| might noh | wud'na | naah goh | kyaah | mos'n |

1. _____
2. _____
3. _____
4. _____
5. _____
6. _____
7. _____
8. _____

9. _____
10. _____

Practice Exercise 35

Translate the Jamaican Creole Sentences from Practice Exercise 34 to English.

1. _____
2. _____
3. _____
4. _____
5. _____
6. _____
7. _____
8. _____
9. _____
10. _____

Practice Exercise 36

Underline the negative modal auxiliary verbs in the following sentences, and then rewrite the sentences in English.

1. Mi cud'na did si di ᴱtruck a ᴱcome.

   _____

2. ᴱJerome wi noh pyeh di ᴱbill ᶠif yuh noh ᴱremind im.

   _____

3. Mi faada naah goh ᴱtravel goh ᴱabroad nex samma.

   _____

4. Dem wud'na ᴱcome ᴱif dem neva did ha wau kyaar.

   _____

5. Mi bredda kyaah ^Efix di kyaar, soh im aggo tek ih goh a di ^Emechanic.

_____

6. Wi ^Eparents dem seh wi noh fi ^Ecome huom lyet.

_____

7. Deeh cud'n ^Ecome pan ^Etime.

_____

8. ^EAliesha shud'na did spen soh ^Emuch ^Etime a ^Etalk wid aar fren dem, bikaah ^Enow shi lyet fi wok.

_____

9. If ^Jyuh ^Jnoh buy ^Jdi book now, ^Jyuh ^Jwi ^Jnoh come back come ^Jsi it.

_____

10. Di sing_ja naah goh perfaam a di shuo.

_____

Practice Exercise 37

Use the following words and the negative modal auxiliary verbs previously discussed to form sentences in Jamaican Creole. Identify the part of speech of the word you used by writing it on the line (e.g. noun, verb, etc.).

aatis *n.* artist　　**faati leg** *n.* millipede
badlokid *adj.* unlucky　　**farid** *n.* forehead
bakk'l *n., v.* bottle　　**jaah weh** *v. phrase* pull away; move away
craap *n., v.* scratch

1. _____

　　Part of speech _____

2. _____

   Part of speech _____

3. _____

   Part of speech _____

4. _____

   Part of speech _____

5. _____

   Part of speech _____

6. _____

   Part of speech _____

7. _____

   Part of speech _____

Asking Questions

Questions are used to request information, and a question mark is used to punctuate the sentence. When a question is asked in English, an adverb (such as *where, when, how, why,* etc.), a pronoun (such as *who* or *whose*), a modal auxiliary verb (such as *can, will,* etc.), or the verb *be* is used to begin the sentence. For example:

When is he leaving?

Who said that?

Can you believe what happened?

Are you going to the wedding with your friend?

How Questions Are Formed in Jamaican Creole

In Jamaican Creole, questions are structured like statements, where the subject is stated first. For example:

Jamaican Creole	English
Iona deh ya?	lit. Iona is here?
	(*Is Iona here?*)
Yuh nuo wa mi mean?	lit. You know what I mean?
	(*Do you know what I mean?*)
How dem fi duh dat?	lit. How they should do that?
	(*How can they do that?*)

The Verb Bi

In English, the verb *be* is used in some cases to begin a question. An example is *Are you a nurse?* In Jamaican Creole, the subject always comes before the verb as if one were making a statement. For example:

Jamaican Creole	English
Di paati <u>a did</u> laas night?	lit. The party <u>was</u> last night?
	(*Was the party last night?*)
When im <u>did deh</u> a wok?	lit. When he <u>was</u> at work?
	(*When was he at work?*)
Yuh <u>a plan fi clean</u>?	lit. You <u>are planning to clean</u>?
	(*Are you planning to clean?*)

When the Verb Bi Indicates Location

When the verb *bi* is used in a question to ask about the location or position of the subject, the formation of the verb depends on the tense of the sentence.

Here are examples of the use of the verb *bi* in questions formed in the present, past, and future tense:

Jamaican Creole	English
Weh di puppy <u>deh</u>?	lit. Where the puppy <u>is</u>?
	(*Where is the puppy?*)
Di book dem <u>did deh</u> a di store?	lit. The books <u>were</u> at the store?
	(*Were the books at the store?*)
Dem <u>aggo deh deh</u>?	lit. They <u>are going to be</u> there?
	(*Will they be there?*)

Note that the verb is sometimes omitted when the location or position of a noun is being inquired about in the simple present tense of Jamaican Creole:

Example 1. *Weh yuh madda?* (E. *Where is your mother?*)

Example 2. *Weh dem girl?* (E. *Where are the/those girls?*)

Note that *deh* is not omitted when the location or position of a pronoun is being inquired about. An example of this is *Weh im deh?* (E. lit. *Where he is?/Where is he?*).

The Verb Bi and Adjectives

When an adjective is used with the verb *bi* in a sentence, the verb is formed based on the tense being used. For example:

Jamaican Creole	English
Elain <u>did</u> taiyad?	Lit. Elaine <u>was</u> tired?
	(Was Elaine tired?)
Di ruod foggy?	The road <u>is</u> foggy?
	(Is the road foggy?)
Di door <u>neva</u> cluoz?	The door <u>wasn't</u> closed?
	(Wasn't the door closed?)

The Verb Bi and Adverbs

When an adverb such as E. *when,* E. *how,* E. *why,* *wa* (E. *what),* or E. *which,* or a pronoun such as E. *who,* *fuu* (E. *whose),* or *fihuu* (E. *whose)* is used to inquire about the subject of the sentence, the verb can be:

1. Used in the base infinitive form *bi.*
In this case, the subject and the object of the sentence are placed before the verb. *Aggo, beeh, did, weeh, wi,* and *wudda, etc.* are used with the verb to indicate the tense. For example:

Jamaican Creole	English
When dat <u>bi</u>?	lit. When that <u>is</u>?
	(When is that?)
Who dem <u>beeh bi</u>?	lit. Who they <u>were</u>?
	(Who were they?)
Wa dat <u>did bi</u>?	lit. What that <u>was</u>?
	(What was that?)

2. Omitted from the sentence altogether in the simple present tense. For example:

Jamaican Creole	English
Fihuu dat?	lit. Whose that?
	(*Whose is that?*)
Wa demya?	lit. What these?
	(*What are these?*)
Fuu dis?	lit. Whose this?
	(*Whose is this?*)

Note that *rule 2* (omitting the verb) does not apply when *ih* or *it* is used before or after the verb. In these cases, *rule 1* or *rule 3* is followed where the verb is not omitted. An example of this is *Wa ih bi?* (lit. *What it is?*/E. *What is it?*).

3. Or it is conjugated *a* or *a did* (also used as *a beeh, a weeh, a beeh did, or a weeh did*) and is used at the beginning of the sentence. For example:

Jamaican Creole	English
<u>A did</u> which one dat?	lit. <u>It was</u> which one that?
	(*Which one was that?*)
<u>A</u> fuu disya?	lit. <u>It is</u> whose this?
	(*Whose is this?*)
<u>A did</u> wa datdeh?	lit. <u>It was</u> what that?
	(*What was that?*)

Sometimes Jamaicans add *a* at the beginning of questions. This is mainly done for emphasis. It would seem like a version of the passive voice. For example:

Jamaican Creole	English
<u>A</u> where him did deh?	lit. <u>It is</u> where he was?
	(*Where was he?*)
<u>A</u> who did seh soh?	lit. <u>It is</u> who had said so?
	(*Who had said so?*)
<u>A</u> when dem a come?	lit. <u>It is</u> when they are coming?
	(*When are they coming?*)

Practice Exercise 38

Translate the following questions to Jamaican Creole.

1. Will you be at the birthday party in December?

   _____

2. Is she your friend?

   _____

3. Do you like to dance?

   _____

4. Are Keisha and Terrisha sisters?

   _____

5. How long will the electricity company take to reconnect the electricity?

   _____

6. Can he drop me off at home, and will you be there when I arrive?

   _____

7. When is the exam, and how soon will we know the result?

   _____

8. Can I have some crackers with my tea?

   _____

9. Who will help us with the application?

   _____

10. Does she visit her grandparents in the country?

    _____

Practice Exercise 39

Translate the following questions to English.

1. A weh di ^Ebus ^Estop deh?

   _____

2. ^EHow mi kyah fain di puos ^Eoffice?

   _____

3. Weh yuh did deh yessideh, an weh yuh aggo deh ^Etomorrow?

   _____

4. ^EPaula naah goh wid wi a ^EMandeville agen?

   _____

5. Yuh kyah gi mi sooh ^Ejuice inna wau ^Eglass?

   _____

6. ^EWhen dem aggo pyent di ^Ewall an ^Efix di ^Efurniture dem weh brok-op?

   _____

7. ^JA who ^Ja cook ^Jdinna tonight?

   _____

8. ^EHow ^Elong yuh aggo deh deh, an ^Ehow ^Elong mi fi wyet pan yuh?

   _____

9. Di govana did ^Evisit di ^Ecity laas iyer?

   _____

10. ^EWhich ^Eone a fiyuh, an ^Ewhich ^Eone a fimmi?

   _____

Practice Exercise 40

Use the following lines to write your own Jamaican Creole questions.

1. _____
2. _____
3. _____
4. _____
5. _____
6. _____
7. _____
8. _____
9. _____
10. _____

Practice Exercise 41

Translate the questions you formed in Practice Exercise 40 to English.

1. _____
2. _____
3. _____
4. _____
5. _____
6. _____
7. _____
8. _____
9. _____
10. _____

Practice Exercise 42

Transform the following statements into Jamaican Creole questions.

1. We are going to the school dinner on Saturday.

   _____

2. Francine bought a bus ticket on her way from work.

   _____

3. Missy told them that she would not be home early tonight.

   _____

4. It will be a sunny day tomorrow.

   _____

5. The mango is ripe when the skin turns yellow.

   _____

6. On Heroes Day, the students will be helping to plant trees in the schoolyard.

   _____

7. The children know how to complete their assignment.

   _____

8. They speak Spanish in Cuba.

   _____

9. The boy knows how to play the piano and the trumpet.

   _____

10. We will eat lunch at one pm today because we ate a late breakfast.

   _____

Practice Exercise 43

Use the following words to form questions in Jamaican Creole. Identify the part of speech of the word you used by writing it on the line (e.g. noun, verb, etc.).

baan *adj.* born   **noh'n** *adv., n.* nothing
chrip *v.* strip   **sooweh** *adv.* somewhere
en *n., v.* end   **waa/wa** a *contr.* what is
haad *adj., adv.* hard

1. _____

   Part of speech _____

2. _____

   Part of speech _____

3. _____

   Part of speech _____

4. _____

   Part of speech _____

5. _____

   Part of speech _____

6. _____

   Part of speech _____

7. _____

   Part of speech _____

Showing Ownership

The methods of showing ownership in English and Jamaican Creole are similar. A discussion of possessive pronouns, possessive adjectives, and possessive nouns follows.

The Possessive Pronouns

A possessive pronoun shows ownership and stands in place of a noun. The following possessive pronouns are used to show ownership in Jamaican Creole and English.

Possessive Pronouns

Person	Jamaican Creole	English
First (sing.)	fimmi	mine
Second (sing.)	fiyuh	yours
Third (sing.)	fihim	his
	fiar	hers
	fiit/fihit	its
First (plur.)	fiwi	ours
Second (plur.)	fiunnu/fuunu	yours
Third (plur.)	fidem	theirs

The possessive pronouns of Jamaican Creole are used in a similar manner as in English. For example:

Jamaican Creole	English
A <u>fihim</u>.	It is <u>his</u>.
Di pink book a <u>fimmi</u>.	The pink book is <u>mine</u>.
Di yellow pen a <u>fiar</u>.	The yellow pen is <u>hers</u>.

The Use of Uon with Possessive Pronouns in Jamaican Creole

In Jamaican Creole, *uon* (E. *own*) is sometimes used along with the possessive pronoun to indicate ownership. For example:

Jamaican Creole	English
Dem a <u>fihim uon</u>.	lit. They are <u>his own</u>.
	(*They are his.*)
Di big house a <u>fiar uon</u>.	lit. The big house is <u>her own</u>.
	(*The big house is hers.*)
A <u>fidem uon</u>.	lit. It is <u>their own</u>.
	(*It is theirs.*)

Possessive Adjectives

Possessive adjectives demonstrate a relationship of possession or ownership between people, animals, and things by showing which is owned or possessed by the other. The possessive adjectives are used in a similar manner in Jamaican Creole and English.

Possessive Adjectives

Person	Jamaican Creole	English
First (sing.)	mi/fimmi	my
Second (sing.)	yuh/fiyuh	your
Third (sing.)	iih/im/fihim	his
	aar/fiar	her
	ih/fiit/fihit	its
First (plur.)	wi/fiwi	our
Second (plur.)	unnu/fiunnu/fuunu	your
Third (plur.)	deeh/dem/fidem	their

Examples of the use of possessive adjectives:

Jamaican Creole	English
A <u>fiyuh book</u>.	It is <u>your book</u>.
<u>Ih wing</u> ben.	<u>Its wing</u> is bent.
A <u>fiwi daag</u> did dig di huol.	It is <u>our dog</u> [that] dug the hole.

In Jamaican Creole, possessive adjectives that begin with *fi* (such as *fimmi, fiyuh, fihim*, etc.) are more emphatic or demonstrate a stronger connection to the thing possessed than do the others (such as *mi, yuh, im*, etc.). This is especially true if one is demonstrating how one is related to another person. So, if one were to say *A mi bredda* (E. *It is my brother*), the level of possessiveness is lower or less emphatic than if one were to say *A fimmi bredda*.

The Possessive Nouns

Like possessive adjectives, possessive nouns show a relationship of possession or ownership between two nouns.

In English, possession is communicated by adding *'s* or *'* to the noun. Examples include *the boys' schools* and *Kerona's room*.

In Jamaican Creole, there are three ways to show a relationship of possession between nouns:

1. No addition is made to the noun. The two nouns are merely stated one behind the other, and it is understood that the first mentioned noun possesses or owns the second. For example:

Jamaican Creole	English
Mi <u>madda cat</u> jump chruu di winda.	My <u>mother's cat</u> jumped through the window.
<u>Misha sista</u> walk wid aar to school.	<u>Misha's sister</u> walks with her to school.
<u>Neisha bag</u> drop.	<u>Neisha's bag</u> dropped/fell.

2. *A fi* is used before the noun to mean *it is for*. For example:

Jamaican Creole	English
A <u>fi</u> Shara.	lit. It is for Shara.
	(*It is Shara's.*)
Di biscuit <u>a fi</u> di byebi.	lit. The biscuit is for the baby.
	(*The biscuit is the baby's.*)
Di mango dem <u>a fi</u> Missa Clarke.	lit. The mangoes are for Mr. Clarke.
	(*The mangoes are Mr. Clarke's.*)

3. *Uon* is placed after the noun. For example:

Jamaican Creole	English
A <u>Lamar uon</u>.	lit. It is <u>Lamar's own</u>.
	(*It is Lamar's*).
Dem a di <u>pikni uon</u>.	lit. They are the <u>child's own</u>.
	(*They are the child's.*)
Di orange a di <u>man uon</u>.	lit. The orange is the <u>man's own</u>.
	(*The orange is the man's.*)

Sometimes there is a combination of formations 2 and 3, where *a fi* and *uon* are used with the noun. For example:

Jamaican Creole	English
A <u>fi</u> Lamar <u>uon</u>.	lit. It <u>is for</u> Lamar's <u>own</u>.
	(*It is Lamar's.*)
Dem <u>a fi</u> di pikni <u>uon</u>.	lit. They <u>are for</u> the child's <u>own</u>.
	(*They are the child's.*)
It <u>a fi</u> di man <u>uon</u>.	lit. It <u>is for</u> the man's <u>own</u>.
	(*It is the man's.*)

Practice Exercise 44

Translate the following sentences to Jamaican Creole.

1. The house across the road is Marsha's and her family's.

    _____

2. Petrina's dog is black and brown.

    _____

3. Our school is located in Manchester, but we live in Clarendon.

    _____

4. My sweater is hanging on the door.

    _____

5. Her aunt's sister is the principal of the school.

    _____

6. The shoes belong to my sister.

    _____

7. The man will be taking his child to school.

    _____

8. The car is mine.

    _____

9. His trip was cancelled because a storm is coming.

    _____

10. The celebrity's house is large and fancy.

    _____

Practice Exercise 45

Translate the following sentences to English.

1. Mi fren an ^ETrudy sista goh a di syem ^Eschool, ^Ebut dem ^Elive inna diffrent plyes.

   _____

2. Datdeh ^Ebook deh a fimmi.

   _____

3. A fi ^EDemar uon.

   _____

4. ^EMona kyaar ha nof ^Escratch pan ih bikaah shi lik ih ^Eup inna di ^Ewall.

   _____

5. Mi faada ^Eput ^Efive dalla inna mi ^Epiggybank.

   _____

6. ^EJeremy sista ^Etell wi seh im ^Egone a farin gaah ^Elive.

   _____

7. Fidem ^Eplan naah goh wok.

   _____

8. Di ^Ered ^Eone a fimmi uon.

   _____

9. ^JA ^Jfi John shirt.

   _____

10. A fihuu ^Elaptop deh pan di ^Ebed?

   _____

Practice Exercise 46

Fill in the blanks with the correct possessive adjective, possessive noun, possessive pronoun, or an appropriate word or phrase. The sentence should show possession in some form.

1. ^EGreta ^Etell mi seh shi aggo spen ^Etime wid _____inna ^EBull ^EBay.

2. Di ^Estudent dem aggo styeh bihain afta _____ ^Eclass oova tudeh.

3. Shi ^Eannounce ^Eto _____fren dem an _____ ^Efamily seh shi aggo ^Eretire a di en a di iyer.

4. Di ^Eball a _____ di pikini dem weh ^Elive nex ^Edoor.

5. ^EJeffrey _____dem inna _____ ^Ebag.

6. _____ ^Eroom dotti, soh mi aggo ^Eclean ih.

7. ^JDi yellow dress _____, but ^Jdi blue one _____.

8. _____ nyem dem deh pan dem nyem ^Etag.

9. Dem ^Emix ^Eup wi letta dem an put dem inna _____.

10. ^EKim fuol _____an ^Eput dem inna di ^Ecloset.

Practice Exercise 47

Translate the sentences you formed in Practice Exercise 46 to English.

1. _____
2. _____
3. _____
4. _____
5. _____
6. _____
7. _____

8. _____

9. _____

10. _____

Practice Exercise 48

Indicate whether the following sentences contain possessive adjectives, possessive nouns, or possessive pronouns by underlining the word or words demonstrating possession.

1. He was ordered by the judge to pay a fine.
2. Clinton wrote his essay on the way to school this morning.
3. No one told us that the concert was cancelled.
4. I have my own boat that I use to go fishing up the river.
5. Kamisha's nephew goes to my high school, but we are in different grades.
6. The benches have been painted to protect them from the rain.
7. The workman has been taking a long time to build his house.
8. My mother placed her glass of water on the kitchen counter.
9. We will need to pack our bags for our trip.
10. The stairs are hard to climb.

Practice Exercise 49

Use the following words to form sentences showing ownership in Jamaican Creole. Identify the part of speech of the word you used by writing it on the line (e.g. noun, verb, etc.).

bakk'l *n., v.* bottle

hoks *n., v.* hack; husk

kaad *n.* cord

lakka dat *adv.* like that

naiz *n.* noise

obyeh *v.* obey

ruop *n., v.* rope

1. _____

   Part of speech _____

2. _____

   Part of speech _____

3. _____

   Part of speech _____

4. _____

   Part of speech _____

5. _____

   Part of speech _____

6. _____

   Part of speech _____

7. _____

   Part of speech _____

Forming Adjectives and Adverbs

Adjectives

An adjective is a word that describes a characteristic, state, mood, or some other aspect of a noun or pronoun. Some examples of English adjectives include:

windy	tender
beautiful	caring
angry	wet
rough	dry
patchy	red

Here are some examples of how they are used in English:

It is windy and wet outside today.

Henry is a caring person.

She drives a red car.

The road is rough.

How Adjectives Are Used in Jamaican Creole

Adjectives are used similarly in English and Jamaican Creole. However, there are small differences with usage.

The Verb Bi and Adjectives

The Jamaican Creole verb *bi* behaves irregularly before adjectives and is usually omitted before them. In English, the verb *be* is always used when it occurs before adjectives. Here are some examples:

Jamaican Creole	English
Daniesha <u>tall</u>.	lit. Daniesha <u>tall</u>.
	(Daniesha is tall.)
The jaiv-wyeh <u>wet</u>.	lit. The driveway <u>wet</u>.
	(The driveway is wet.)
Di jerk puok <u>did tenda</u>.	The jerk pork <u>was tender</u>.

Repetition of Adjectives for Emphasis

Jamaicans sometimes repeat adjectives for emphasis. For example:

Jamaican Creole	English
Mi <u>happy happy</u> fi it.	I am [very] <u>happy</u> for it.
Wi house did <u>tiny tiny</u> when mi young.	Our house was [very] <u>tiny</u> when I was young.
Aar dress did <u>muddy muddy</u> yessideh.	Her dress was [very] <u>muddy</u> yesterday.

Adjectives with Dependent Repetition

Certain adjectives (for e.g., *fengkeh-fengkeh* (E. *weak*), *likki-likki* (E. *greedy*), and *nyami-nyami* (E. *greedy*) are adjectives that have a 'dependence' on repetition. This means that if used as a single word, the word would be meaningless. This can be termed a *dependent repetition*. These words are usually not being repeated for emphasis. In English, adjectives are usually not repeated.

Adjectives That Require –Ed

Consistent with the present perfect and past perfect tense of Jamaican Creole, words that require *-ed* to form their adjectives in English are usually not changed in Jamaican Creole. For example:

Jamaican Creole	English
Di likk'l girl <u>muo determine</u>.	The little girl is <u>more determined</u>.
Shi <u>styehshan</u> inna Montego Bay.	She is <u>stationed</u> in Montego Bay.
Di grass <u>cova</u> wid waata.	The grass is <u>covered</u> with water.

The Comparative and Superlative Degrees of Adjectives

The Comparative and Superlative Degrees of English

In English, the comparative degree is used when comparing two people or things. *Er* or *more* is used with the adjective to form the comparative degree. Some examples of this include:

prettier	more beautiful
longer	more joyful
shorter	more energetic
greater	more understanding
fainter	more serious

In English, the superlative degree is used when comparing more than two people or things. *Est* or *most* is used with the adjective to form the superlative degree.

prettiest	most beautiful
longest	most joyful
shortest	most energetic
greatest	most understanding
faintest	most serious

The Comparative and Superlative Degrees of Jamaican Creole

Generally speaking, comparative adjectives arc used similarly in Jamaican Creole and English. In the comparative degree of Jamaican Creole, *a* is used in place of *er,* and *muo* is used in place of *more*. For the superlative degree of Jamaican Creole, *is* or *es* is used in place of *est,* and *muos* is used in place of *most.*

The rules governing the use of the comparative degree and the superlative degree are not very strict in Jamaican Creole. So, you will find that people will use the comparative degree or superlative degree to compare two people or things, or to compare more than two people or things.

Here are some examples of the comparative degree:

Jamaican Creole	English
Disya pen <u>langa</u> dan da one deh.	This pen is <u>longer</u> than that one there.
Janet <u>muo serious</u> dau Donna.	Janet is <u>more serious</u> than Donna.
Di daag <u>bigga</u> dan di cat.	The dog is <u>bigger</u> than the cat.

The comparative adjectives that are irregular in English are also irregular in Jamaican Creole. They include:

JC.	bad	wos	wos
E.	bad	worse	worst

JC.	good	betta	bes
E.	good	better	best

JC.	likk'l	less	liis
E.	little	less	least

JC.	many	muo	muos
E.	many	more	most

JC.	much	muo	muos
E.	much	more	most

Here are some examples of the superlative degree:

Jamaican Creole	English
Terry-Ann a di <u>bes</u> daansa.	Terry-Ann is the <u>best</u> dancer.
Mi madda a di <u>muos determine</u> sumaddi weh mi nuo.	My mother is the <u>most determined</u> person I know.
Out a di four runn‚a dem, Trisha a di <u>faasis</u>.	Out of the four runners, Trisha is the <u>fastest</u>.

Adverbs

An adverb describes how something is done, the degree to which something is done, the intensity of a state, etc. It can give information about verbs, adjectives, or other adverbs. Many adverbs end in -ly, though this is not always the case. Examples of English adverbs are:

prettily	well
happily	fast
slowly	rather
increasingly	still
quickly	soon

How Adverbs Are Used in Jamaican Creole

There are slight differences with the use of adverbs in Jamaican Creole and the use of adverbs in English. Those adverbs that end in *–ly* in English are usually used without–ly in Jamaican Creole. For example:

Jamaican Creole	English
She did sing di song <u>beautiful</u>.	She had sung the song <u>beautifully</u>.
Mi fall asleep <u>quick</u>.	I fall asleep <u>quickly</u>.
Di pikni dem walk <u>sluo</u> pan di sidewalk.	The children walk <u>slowly</u> on the sidewalk.

Repetition of Adverbs

Jamaicans have a tendency to repeat adverbs for emphasis. This is especially true when an action took place in some extraordinary manner. For example:

Jamaican Creole	English
Di byebi talk <u>plyen plyen</u>.	The baby talks [very] plainly.
The bus reach Morant Bay <u>quick quick</u>.	The bus reached Morant Bay [very] quickly.
Di line a move <u>sluo sluo</u>.	The line is moving [very] slowly.

Omitting the Adverb

Jamaicans sometimes avoid using adverbs in sentences. Instead, they choose to construct the sentence in such a way that it does not require an adverb. For example:

Instead Of Saying	One Might Say	English Translation
The children chat noisily.	Di pikni dem naizi.	The children are noisy.
Something is terribly wrong.	So'mn wrong, man.	Something is wrong, man.
He accepted it happily.	Iih did happy fi aksep ih.	He was happy to accept it.

Comparing Adverbs

In English, the comparative degree is usually formed by adding *er* or using *more* with the adverb. Examples of the comparative degree include:

faster	more quickly
earlier	more vigorously
later	more slowly
longer	more plainly
better	more carefully

The superlative degree of English is usually formed by adding *est* or using *most* with the adverb. Examples of the superlative degree include:

fastest	most quickly
earliest	most vigorously
latest	most slowly
longest	most plainly
best	most carefully

Comparing Jamaican Creole Adverbs

The Comparative Degree

In Jamaican Creole, the comparative degree is formed by adding *a* or using *muo*. For example:

Jamaican Creole	English
Disya byebi talk <u>plyena</u> dan di adda pikini.	This baby talks <u>more plainly</u> than the other child.
Di bus reach Morant Bay <u>faasa</u> dan di kyaar.	The bus reached Morant Bay <u>faster than the car</u>.
Dis line yasso a move <u>muo sluo</u> dan dat one.	This line here is moving <u>more slowly</u> than that one.

Sometimes the comparative degree formed by *a* in Jamaican Creole is used in place of the one formed by *muo*. For example:

Instead Of Saying	One Might Say
Shelly reacted <u>more quickly</u> than the other runners.	Shelly riak <u>quick_ia</u> dan di adda runn_ia dem.
I see it <u>more clearly</u> now.	Mi siit <u>clear_ia</u> now.
The bike is moving <u>more slowly</u> than the bus.	Di bike a move <u>slow_ia</u> dan the bus.

The Superlative Degree

In Jamaican Creole, the superlative degree is formed by adding *is* or *es* to the adverb. The superlative degree that is formed by adding *most* in English is not used in Jamaican Creole. Jamaicans typically would not say, for example, *Janice did dance muos gracefully* (E. *Janice danced most gracefully*) unless they are speaking English. Here are examples of the superlative degree:

Jamaican Creole	English
Wi did arrive deh di <u>lyetis</u>.	We arrived there the <u>latest</u>.
Di cherry gum laas <u>langes</u>.	The cherry gum lasts <u>longest</u>.
Gerad iht <u>faases</u>.	Gerad eats <u>fastest</u>.

The comparative adverbs that are irregular in English are also irregular in Jamaican Creole. They include:

JC.	bad	wos	wos
E.	badly	worse	worst

JC.	far	fara	fares
E.	far	farther	farthest

JC.	lyet	lyeta	laas
E.	late	later	last

JC.	much	muo	muos
E.	much	more	most

JC.	well	betta	bes
E.	well	better	best

Practice Exercise 50

Translate the following sentences to Jamaican Creole, and underline the adjectives and/or adverbs in the sentences.

1. She is more hard-working now than when she was younger.

   _____

2. The car sped quickly around the corner.

   _____

3. Ms. Rita is the best music teacher in the school.

   _____

4. My sister is the most caring person I know.

   _____

5. The child walked slowly to school.

   _____

6. Kadeen is better at Chemistry than she is at Biology.

   _____

7. We knew the governor really well.

   _____

8. Simone danced gracefully to the music.

   _____

9. This radio station plays the best music.

   _____

10. Wendy is happiest when she is with her family.

    _____

Practice Exercise 51

Underline the adjectives and adverbs in the following sentences.

1. Di ᴱline did ᴱlong ᴱlong, soh wi nebba badda ᴱbuy di ᴱgrocery dem.

2. Di byebi seh di wod dem plyen plyen.

3. Di likk'l bwuay muo ᴱadventurous dan im ᴱbig bredda.

4. Di flowaz dem ᴱlook wishi-washi.

5. Wi a ᴱwalk faas bikaah wi noh wau di ryen fi ketch wi pan di ruod.

6. Di wokman dem a wok ᴱsteady pan di ᴱhouse frau dis maanin.

7. ᴱKeniel a di tallⱼis ᴱone inna di ᴱgroup.

8. ᴶDi girl ᴶlikk'l but ᴶshi courageous.

9. Tings wi ᴱget betta ᴱonce wi ᴱput di ᴱplan in plyes.

10. Di ᴱdress ᴱlong an colaful, ᴱbut mi noh ᴱlike ih.

Practice Exercise 52

Translate the sentences from Practice Exercise 51 to English.

1. _____

2. _____

3. _____

4. _____

5. _____

6. _____

7. _____

8. _____

9. _____

10. _____

Practice Exercise 53

Underline the adjectives and/or adverbs in the following sentences.

1. Di ᴱpoliceman ᴱrun afta di tiif inna di ryeni wedda.

2. ᴱKenisha ha wau ᴱgood ᴱsinging vais.

3. Di ᴱtree dem a ᴱsway ᴱgentle inna di back‚yaad ᴱbecause a di ᴱbreeze.

4. Shi ᴱdetermine seh shi aggo ᴱstudy an ᴱpass ᴱall a aar ᴱexam dem.

5. ᴱShantana ᴱhappy seh shi a di fos ᴱone fi ᴱfinish aar ryes.

6. Mi wau wau ᴱblue ᴱdress fi ᴱwear goh a di fyer.

7. ᴱPretina muo ᴱapproachable dan aar coz'n.

8. Mi sista ha wau betta andastandin a di ᴱtopic ᴱnow dat shi ᴱstudy.

9. Ih ᴱwindy an ryeni tudeh, soh wi aggo ᴱwalk faas goh huom.

10. Di ᴱshop ᴱbusy an ᴱcrowded pan di week‚en.

Practice Exercise 54

Use the following lines to create your own English sentences containing adjectives and adverbs. Underline all adjectives and adverbs in your sentences.

1. _____

2. _____

3. _____

4. _____

5. _____

6. _____

7. _____

8. _____

9. _____

10. _____

Practice Exercise 55

Use the following words as adjectives or adverbs to form sentences in Jamaican Creole. Identify whether the word was used as an adjective or adverb by writing it on the line.

braalin *adj.* rowdy
fengkeh-fengkeh *adj.* weak
likki-likki *adj.* greedy
lyet *adj., adv.* late

maaga *adj., v.* slim
puo *adj.* poor
tik *adj., adv., n., v.* stick; thick

1. _____

Part of speech _____

2. _____

Part of speech _____

3. _____

Part of speech _____

4. _____

Part of speech _____

5. _____

Part of speech _____

6. _____

Part of speech _____

7. _____

Part of speech _____

Da, Datdeh, Dat, Seh, and Weh

The English word *that* is used as an adjective, adverb, conjunction, and pronoun. Here are some examples of how *that* is used in English:

Adjective	*That house on the left is Mr. Brown's home.*
Adverb	*I did not know he was that good at playing the guitar.*
Conjunction	*I did not believe that he would be leaving so soon.*
Pronoun	*That was the happiest day of our lives.*

There are five words in Jamaican Creole whose meanings translate to *that* in English. They are *da, datdeh, dat, seh*, and *weh*.

Da

Da is used only as an adjective that is followed by a noun:

e.g., *Yuh look like <u>da uhman</u> pan di shuo.* (E. *You look like <u>that woman</u> on the show*).

It can be used to point out a noun somewhere in the distance:

e.g., *Yuh nuo <u>da bwuay</u> oova dehsoh?* (E. *You know <u>that boy</u> over there?*).

When used with *deh, dyer, dehsoh*, and *dyersoh, da* means *that*. When used with *ya* and *yasso*, it means *this*. These pronouns are used to indicate the specific location of the subject:

e.g., *Yuh si <u>da house ya</u>?* (E. *You see <u>this house here</u>?*).

Datdeh

Datdeh identifies a thing. It is used as an adjective or pronoun.

Datdeh as an Adjective

Datdeh can be used as an adjective when followed by a noun. Here are examples of datdeh when used as an adjective:

Jamaican Creole	English
Datdeh purse a fiar.	That purse is hers.
A who datdeh one fa?	lit. It is who that one is for?
	(*Who is that one for?*)
Shi did goh datdeh time.	She had gone that time.

Deh, *dehsoh*, and *dyersoh* are frequently added after the noun referred to by *datdeh* to indicate the specific location of the subject (usually at a distance). For example:

Jamaican Creole	English
Datdeh purse deh a fiar.	That purse there is hers.
A who datdeh one dehsoh fa?	lit. It is who that one right there is for?
	(*Who is that one right there for?*)
Shi did goh datdeh time dyer.	She had gone that time there.
	(*She had gone that time.*)

Datdeh as a Pronoun

Datdeh can be used as a pronoun. It is not, however, used as a relative pronoun that is equivalent to *which* or *who* (such as *money that my cousin sent to her*). Examples of how *datdeh* is used:

Jamaican Creole	English
Datdeh a fidem.	That is theirs.
A wa datdeh?	lit. It is what that?
	(*What is that?*)
Gi him datdeh.	Give him that.

Deh, *dyer*, *dehsoh*, and *dyersoh* are frequently added after *datdeh* to indicate the specific location of the subject. For example:

Jamaican Creole	English
Datdeh dehsoh a fidem.	That right there is theirs.
A wa datdeh dyersoh?	lit. It is what that there?
	(*What is that there?*)
Giim datdeh dehsoh.	Give him that right there.

Dat

Dat is used interchangeably with E. *that* as an adjective, adverb, conjunction, and pronoun. Examples of how *dat* is used:

Jamaican Creole	English
Ih did soh far dat wi aalmuos give up.	It was so far that we almost gave up.
Wi huop dat unnu aggo come fi wau visit.	We hope that you will come for a visit.
A di cat did duh dat.	It was the cat that did that.

When used as an adjective or pronoun, *deh*, *dyer*, *dehsoh*, and *dyersoh* are frequently added after *dat* or after the noun being referred to by *dat* to indicate the specific location or position of the subject. For example:

Jamaican Creole	English
Dat tickit dyer a fidem.	That ticket there is theirs.
A wa datdeh dyersoh?	lit. It is what that there?
	(*What is that there?*)
Giim datdeh deh.	Give him that there.

Seh

Seh is used as a conjunction. It is used after a clause expressing a fact, belief, wish, hope, expectation, opinion, decision, or some feeling/emotion:

e.g., *Wi nuo seh iih did win wau prize* (E. *We knew that he won a prize*).

When the verb *seh* (E. *say*) is used before the conjunction *seh*, the conjunction *seh* is omitted:

e.g., *Shi did seh im a aar fren.* (E. *She had said [that] he is her friend*).

Weh

Weh is used as a relative pronoun that is equivalent to *which* or *who* in usage.

e.g., *Jerome inna di group weh upkeep di campus* (E. *Jerome is in the group that upkeeps the campus*).

Practice Exercise 56

Translate the following sentences to Jamaican Creole.

1. We hope that the child will recover from the flu soon.

    _____

2. The cousins did not live that far apart when they were younger.

    _____

3. That day, we drove across the country.

    _____

4. The purple dress was the one that I wore to the fun day.

    _____

5. His jokes were not that funny, but the crowd laughed anyway.

    _____

6. I believe that it will rain today.

    _____

7. Lina did not know that her brother would be at her graduation.

    _____

8. The book that was on the shelf belongs to my mother.

    _____

9. She did not expect him to do that.

_____

10. He was that close to realizing his dream.

_____

Practice Exercise 57

Identify whether *da, dat, datdeh, seh,* and *weh* are being used as adjective, adverb, conjunction, or pronoun in the following sentences by writing the part of speech on the line.

1. Im a did di ᴱstudent weh ᴱget di high‚es maak pan di ᴱexam.

_____

2. Da ᴱhouse deh weh deh pan di ᴱhill a Maas ᴱPaul ᴱhouse.

_____

3. Datdeh a fi aar faada.

_____

4. A did ong'l yessideh dat wi did a ᴱtalk bout im.

_____

5. Wi neva dat ᴱhungry, ᴱbut wi iht dinna any‚wyeh.

_____

6. Mi did hyeh seh dem aggo ᴱcancel di shuo bikaah di sing‚a kyaah mek ih.

_____

7. ᴱJacky wau di ᴱblack han‚bag weh deh pan di ᴱshelf.

_____

8. Mi coz'n did gi mi datdeh ᴱskirt deh, an den shi gimmi di ᴱblouse fi ᴱmatch.

_____

9. Shi [E]resemble da [E]girl deh inna di [E]movie.

_____

10. Di pikini nuo seh di [E]journey [E]long, [E]but shi [E]still wau goh.

_____

Practice Exercise 58

Translate the sentences from Practice Exercise 57 to English.

1. _____

2. _____

3. _____

4. _____

5. _____

6. _____

7. _____

8. _____

9. _____

10. _____

Practice Exercise 59

Fill in the blanks with the appropriate Jamaican Creole word (*da*, *datdeh*, *seh*, or *weh*). Do not use the word *dat* as it can be used in place of any of the other words. Identify whether *da*, *datdeh*, *seh*, and *weh* are being used as adjective, adverb, conjunction, or pronoun in the following sentences by writing the part of speech on the line below the sentence.

1. Im tink _____ dem kyaah [F]afford fi pyeh dem di [E]money.

_____

2. ^EKenisha ^Ebelieve _____ aar fren naah goh ^Eget fi ^Ebuy di kyek.

_____

3. A _____ ^Emovie aggo staat ^Enow.

_____

4. _____ bus ^Jdeh run ^Jfrau Downtown to Spanish Town.

_____

5. Di ^Echicken dem _____ inna di ^Erefrigerator a fi dinna.

_____

6. Di ^Eemployee cud'n ^Ebelieve _____ a im get soh ^Emuch ^Emoney fi im buonos.

_____

7. ^EJerome did ^Ebring _____ fuon deh fi ^ECharlene.

_____

8. Mi gi mi bredda ^Efifty dalla ^Eout a di ^Emoney _____ mi ^Euncle gi mi.

_____

9. _____ a fi ^EShelly an _____ a fi ^ESheila.

_____

10. Cluos _____ winda deh.

_____

Practice Exercise 60

Translate the sentences from Practice Exercise 59 to English.

1. _____

2. _____

3. _____

4. _____

5. _____

6. _____

7. _____

8. _____

9. _____

10. _____

Practice Exercise 61

Use the following words to form sentences that include either *da*, *datdeh*, *seh*, or *weh* in Jamaican Creole. Identify the part of speech of the word you used by writing it on the line (e.g. adjective, adverb, etc.).

bagabu *n.* caterpillar
blinki *n.* firefly
chi-chi *n.* termite
saach *v.* search

pikni/pikini *n.* child
uhman *n.* woman
ya *adv., n.* here

1. _____

   Part of speech _____

2. _____

   Part of speech _____

3. _____

   Part of speech _____

4. _____

   Part of speech _____

5. _____

   Part of speech _____

6. _____

   Part of speech _____

7. _____

   Part of speech _____

The Tendency to Use Goh and Come after Verbs of Movement

In Jamaican Creole, *goh* and E. *come* are sometimes used after verbs that demonstrate movement (e.g., *walk*, *run*, *ride*, *fly,* and *send*). This verb formation gives the idea that the action leads to some place close (*come*) to the speaker or subject, some place at a distance (*goh*) from the speaker or subject, or from one place to another, depending on the direction of the movement. The use of *goh* and *come* in this manner is unique to Jamaican Creole and is not used in English.

The Use of Goh

Here are some examples of how *goh* is used in Jamaican Creole:

Jamaican Creole	English
Kamisha <u>did run goh</u> a di store fi aar madda.	lit. Kamisha <u>had run go</u> to the store for her mother.
	(*Kamisha had run to the store for her mother.*)
Di man <u>naah walk goh</u> a town.	lit. The man <u>is not walking go</u> to town.
	(*The man is not walking to town.*)
Shi <u>a travel goh</u> huom inna Maach.	lit. She <u>is traveling go</u> home in March.
	(*She is traveling home in March.*)

The Use of Come

Here are some examples of how *come* is used in Jamaican Creole:

Jamaican Creole	English
Simone <u>a run come</u> look fi wi.	lit. Simone <u>is running come</u> look for us.
	(*Simone is coming to see us.*)
Wi <u>did fly come</u> when wi hear.	lit. We <u>flew come</u> when we heard.
	(*We came flying when we heard.*)
Di man <u>a ride bike come</u> a di event.	lit. The man <u>is riding bike come</u> to the event.
	(*The man is riding a bike to the event.*)

When a Noun or Pronoun Occurs Between The Verb and Goh or Come

Sometimes a noun or pronoun (or a noun or pronoun phrase) is inserted between the verb and *goh* or *come*. For example:

Jamaican Creole	English
Shi <u>a move</u> aar family <u>come</u> a di country.	lit. She <u>is moving</u> her family <u>come</u> to the country.
	(*She is moving her family to the country.*)
It <u>deh</u> pan di wyeh <u>goh</u> a Mandeville.	lit. It <u>is</u> on the way <u>go</u> to Mandeville.
	(*It is on the way to Mandeville.*)
Di truck <u>carry</u> plank buod frau May Pen <u>goh</u> a town.	lit. The truck <u>carries</u> plank boards from May Pen <u>go</u> to town.
	(*The truck carries plank boards from May Pen to town.*)

When Goh and Come Indicate the Tense of the Sentence

Sometimes *goh* and *come* are used instead of the main verb to indicate the tense of the sentence. For example:

Jamaican Creole	English
Dem <u>move</u> the store <u>a come</u> a Montego Bay.	lit. They <u>move</u> the store <u>is coming</u> to Montego Bay.
	(*They are moving the store to Montego Bay.*)
Wi <u>deh</u> pan wi wyeh <u>did a goh</u> a di paati.	lit. We <u>are</u> on our way <u>were going</u> to the party.
	(*We were on our way to the party.*)
Di truck <u>carry</u> plank buod frau May Pen <u>a goh</u> a town.	lit. The truck <u>carries</u> plank boards from May Pen <u>is going</u> to town.
	(*The truck is carrying plank boards from May Pen to town.*)

When Goh, Cooh, And Come Are Used To Express Emotion

Goh, *cooh*, and *come* are sometimes used before verbs to express surprise. In these instances, *goh*, *cooh*, and *come* are usually not indicating literal direction or location, although they sometimes do. The verbs they modify are not limited to verbs of movement. Usually, the action or event took place in the recent past. For example:

Jamaican Creole	English
Shelly <u>come tell</u> mi seh shi naah goh.	lit. Shelly <u>come tell</u> me that she is not going.
	(*Shelly told me that she is not going.*)
Mi <u>cooh si</u> aar inna Maroon Town.	lit. I <u>come see</u> her in Maroon Town.
	(*I saw her in Maroon Town.*)
Im <u>come tek over</u> di business.	lit. He <u>come take over</u> the business.
	(*He took over the business.*)

The Use of Jump Goh, Jump Come, Jump Cooh, and Goh

Jump goh, jump come, jump cooh, or *goh* is often used before a verb to suggest that an action was done hurriedly or without consideration. *Jump* is pronounced as in English. In most instances, the action or statement is inappropriate. These phrases most times do not refer to literal direction or physical location. For example:

Jamaican Creole	English
Shi <u>goh put</u> aar bag pan di people dem tyeb'l.	lit. She <u>go put</u> her bag on the people's table.
	(*She [inappropriately] put her bag on someone's table.*)
Kadiesha <u>jump cooh opin</u> di duo, an now di ryen wet di bed.	lit. Kadiesha <u>jump come open</u> the door, and now the rain wet the bed.
	(*Kadeisha opened the door, and now the rain wet the bed.*)
Shi <u>did jump goh finish</u> aar huomwok when aar faada come huom.	lit. She <u>jumped go finish</u> her homework when her father came home.
	(*She [hurriedly] finished her homework when her father came home.*)
Im coz'n <u>jump come seh</u> im fi lef di concert.	lit. His cousin <u>jump come say</u> he should leave the concert.
	(*His cousin said [on a whim/ without consideration] that he should leave the concert.*)

Practice Exercise 62

Translate the following sentences to Jamaican Creole. Use any of the words described in the lesson to show movement, direction, or emotion.

1. The boys traveled to their grandmother's house yesterday.

   _____

2. The cousins hurried to school so they could make it to class on time.

   _____

3. Sasha walked a mile to get water from the shop.

   _____

4. Diana said her friend was wasteful, and now her friend is upset.

   _____

5. He put the book on the shelf, and it fell off.

   _____

6. The birds perched on the fence next to the house.

   _____

7. The dog chased after a mouse in the tall grass.

   _____

8. We are going to take the taxi to the store.

   _____

9. He put the beef in the hot oven, and it burned.

   _____

10. The mother ran after the mischievous girls.

   _____

Practice Exercise 63

Determine whether the underlined part of the sentences below describes movement from one place to another. Write *movement* or *no movement* on the line.

1. Di byebi <u>a ᴱcrawl goh</u> a aar madda.

   _____

2. Marvin <u>run ᴶgoh buy</u> fish ᴶan fruit ᴶa ᴶmaakit.

   _____

3. ᴱMelissa <u>ᴱcome seh</u> wi fi styeh bihain an ᴱclean ᴱup di ᴱroom.

   _____

4. ᴱLetisha <u>ᴱcome ᴱwash</u> aar cluos dem an ᴱgone pan di ruod.

   _____

5. ᴱSuzie <u>a ᴱcarry aar pikini dem goh</u> a di ᴱstudio goh tek ᴱpicture.

   _____

6. Mi <u>a ᴱtry goh ᴱfinish</u> di ᴱlesson bifuo a ᴱtime fi goh a ᴱbed.

   _____

7. ᴱJacky <u>ᴱjump goh sidong</u> pan di ᴱchair an brok ih.

   _____

8. Im faada <u>ᴱcome ᴱfix</u> di ryedio inna im ᴱroom.

   _____

9. ᴱTrisha <u>ᴱjump goh ᴱtell</u> im weh yuh seh, an ᴱnow im ᴱupset.

   _____

10. Shi naah <u>jaiv goh</u> a ᴱSt. Mary bikaah shi aggo tek di ᴱbus.

   _____

Practice Exercise 64

Translate the sentences from Practice Exercise 63 to English.

1. _____

2. _____

3. _____

4. _____

5. _____

6. _____

7. _____

8. _____

9. _____

10. _____

Practice Exercise 65

Use the following subjects to construct your own Jamaican Creole sentences to show either movement or emotion by using *come*, *goh*, *cooh*, *jump goh*, *jump come*, or *jump goh*.

1. Sharon _____

2. Kenisha _____

3. Im _____

4. Di pikini _____

5. Di man _____

6. Shi _____

7. Jerome _____

8. Dem _____

9. Mi _____

10. Gerald _____

Practice Exercise 66

Translate the sentences you formed in Practice Exercise 65 to English.

1. _____
2. _____
3. _____
4. _____
5. _____
6. _____
7. _____
8. _____
9. _____
10. _____

Practice Exercise 67

Construct your own Jamaican Creole sentences to show either movement or emotion by using the following words along with *come, goh, cooh, jump goh, jump come,* or *jump goh.* Identify the part of speech of the word you used by writing it on the line.

dochi *n.* small, round pot

higla *n.* peddler; vendor; a person who sells ground produce in a food market

l ikk'l-muo *adv., inter.* later

maanin *interj., n.* mornin

saadiin *n.* sardine

uov'n *n.* oven

wok *n., v.* work

1. _____

Part of speech _____

2. _____

Part of speech _____

3. _____

Part of speech _____

4. _____

Part of speech _____

5. _____

Part of speech _____

6. _____

Part of speech _____

7. _____

Part of speech _____

Commands

A command is an order. It indicates what someone should do. Commands begin with a verb, and this verb describes how the pronoun (*you*) should act upon another noun or pronoun (e.g., *Take it to her*). It is understood that *you* (pronoun) *take it* (pronoun that should be acted upon) *to her* (pronoun action is directed toward). Here are some English commands:

Allow the children to leave class early today.

Give Nora one of the mangoes and two of the oranges.

Show us the way to the river.

Commands are used in Jamaican Creole as they are in English. The word *please* and/or the name of the person being referred to is sometimes added at the beginning or at the end of the sentence. For example:

Jamaican Creole	English
Please tell Maas Ben son fi come ya.	Please tell Mr. Ben's son to come here.
Gi di gif to aar, please.	Give the gift to her, please.
Goh wid yuh bredda, Nelisha.	Go with your brother, Nelisha.

Commands Involving the Verb Gi

The verb *gi* is generally used in commands as it is in English. For example:

Jamaican Creole	English
<u>Gi</u> aar di fuon fi tek di pikcha.	<u>Give</u> her the phone to take the picture.
<u>Gi</u> him wa due to him.	<u>Give</u> him what is due to him.
<u>Gimmi</u> mi bag.	<u>Give me</u> my bag.

The noun or pronoun that should be acted upon can be omitted if everyone is aware of what object/s should be acted upon. Commands like these are sometimes used informally in English. Look at the following examples:

Jamaican Creole	English
Gi aar.	lit. Give her.
	(Give it/them to her.)
Gimmi.	lit. Give me.
	(Give it/them to me.)
Gi dem.	lit. Give them.
	(Give it/them to them.)
Giim.	lit. Give him.
	(Give it/them to him.)

Sometimes when there are objects being acted upon (plural), *dem* is added at the end of the sentence to communicate this. Look at the following examples:

Jamaican Creole	English
Gi aar <u>dem</u>.	lit. Give her <u>them</u>.
	(Give them to her.)
Gimmi <u>dem</u>.	lit. Give me <u>them</u>.
	(Give them to me.)
Gi dem <u>dem</u>.	lit. Give them <u>them</u>.
	(Give them to them.)
Giim <u>dem</u>.	lit. Give him <u>them</u>.
	(Give them to him.)

Negative Commands

Negative commands state what someone should not do. They begin with the phrase *do not* (*don't*). For example:

Do not play in the busy street.

Do not sit on top of the table.

Do not give them the book.

In Jamaican Creole, *noh*, *dooh*, and *duo* are used in negative commands. They mean *do not* (*don't*). For example:

Jamaican Creole	English
<u>Duo</u> gi dem noh'n.	lit. <u>Don't</u> give them nothing.
	(Don't give them anything.)
<u>Dooh</u> seh soh.	<u>Don't</u> say so.
<u>Noh</u> put di dish dehsoh.	<u>Don't</u> put the dish there.

Negative Compound Commands

A compound command has two independent clauses. When *noh*, *dooh*, and *duo* are used in negative compound commands, both clauses require one of these negative auxiliary verbs. The same format of English, where both clauses require negative auxiliary verbs, is used in Jamaican Creole. Any combination of the words is usually used in Jamaican Creole. For example:

Jamaican Creole	English
<u>Noh</u> goh a di dance, an <u>noh</u> goh a aar house.	<u>Don't</u> go to the dance, and <u>don't</u> go to her house.
<u>Dooh</u> tell yuh sista, an <u>duo</u> tell yuh fren.	<u>Don't</u> tell your sister, and <u>don't</u> tell your friend.
<u>Duo</u> giim di money, an <u>noh</u> gi aar di cheque.	<u>Don't</u> give him the money, and <u>don't</u> give her the cheque.

Practice Exercise 68

Translate the following commands to Jamaican Creole.

1. Show me how to sew the buttons unto the blouse.

   _____

2. Tell me how to get to Ocho Rios by public transportation.

   _____

3. Give Fitzroy some time to finish his assignments before completing his chores.

   _____

4. Pay for your ticket now before they run out.

   _____

5. Remove the vase from the table, and put it on the shelf.

   _____

6. Take the rubbish out before you leave the house in the morning.

   _____

7. Make me a glass of lemonade with fresh lemons.

   _____

8. Start cooking dinner early because we will be leaving for the show in a few hours.

   _____

9. Put all the seasonings on the chicken, and put it in the oven.

   _____

10. Tell her to give you a sample of the product.

    _____

Practice Exercise 69

Translate the following commands to English.

1. Tell Marva ʲfi come ʲya right now.

   _____

2. Lef yuh yaad ᴱearly soh yuh kyah ᴱreach ᴱschool pan ᴱtime.

   _____

3. Sen wau ᴱemail ᴱto yuh ᴱfamily dem fi mek dem nuo seh yuh ᴱfine.

   _____

4. ᴱStop wyes di waata, an ton aaf di ᴱpipe.

   _____

5. Shuo mi yuh pikcha dem weh yuh tek pan yuh ᴱtrip laas iyer.

   _____

6. ᴱFeed di daag an di ᴱcat dem.

   _____

7. ᴱPick ᴱup di pyepa dem aaf di groun, an ᴱput dem inna di ᴱbin.

   _____

8. Noh wyeh yuh sweatʲa ᴱtonight bikaah ih naah goh kuol.

   _____

9. Tek di ᴱdress goh ᴱback a di ᴱstore.

   _____

10. ᴱMove di kyaar ᴱout a di driveʲwyeh.

   _____

Practice Exercise 70

Translate the commands in Practice Exercise 69 to English.

1. _____
2. _____
3. _____
4. _____
5. _____
6. _____
7. _____
8. _____
9. _____
10. _____

Practice Exercise 71

Determine if the following sentences are statements or commands, and then translate the sentences to English.

1. Rimemba fi cluos di ^{E}front duo ^{E}when yuh a goh a ^{E}bed.

   Statement or command _____

   _____

2. ^{E}Jason, mek ^{E}sure yuh ^{E}stop a di ^{E}shop an ^{E}get ^{E}cheese pan di wyeh huom.

   Statement or command _____

   _____

3. ^{E}Dwayne byek di kyek yessideh an ih ^{E}done tudeh.

   Statement or command _____

   _____

4. Shi a ^Ecome fi ^Ecome ^Etell yuh di ^Enews.

   Statement or command _____

   _____

5. Janice ^Jtek ^Jdi new dress out ^Ja ^Jdi bag.

   Statement or command _____

   _____

6. ^ETell mi di chruut.

   Statement or command _____

   _____

7. Wok shi a wok pan di halidyeh.

   Statement or command _____

   _____

8. Gryeta di kuokanat an ^Eput di ^Epeas dem inna di ^Epot pan di stuov.

   Statement or command _____

   _____

9. Bi ^Ehappy seh yuh a styeh huom.

   Statement or command _____

   _____

10. Sidong dem did sidong pan di ^Esidewalk inna di iivlin.

   Statement or command _____

   _____

Practice Exercise 72

Use the following lines to construct English commands.

1. _____
2. _____
3. _____
4. _____
5. _____
6. _____
7. _____
8. _____
9. _____
10. _____

Practice Exercise 73

Use the following words to form commands in Jamaican Creole. Identify the part of speech of the word you used by writing it on the line (e.g. noun, verb, etc.).

ak *n., v.* act   **pongkin** *n.* pumpkin

iyez *n.* ear   **maskita** *n.* mosquito

lik *n., v..* hit   **ruobot** *n., v.* robot; illegal taxi; taxi driver

lyeh *n., v.* lay   operating illegal taxi; to operate a taxi illegally

1. _____

   Part of speech _____

2. _____

   Part of speech _____

3. _____

   Part of speech _____

4. _____

   Part of speech _____

5. _____

   Part of speech _____

6. _____

   Part of speech _____

7. _____

   Part of speech _____

Repetition of Nouns, Pronouns, and Verbs

It was discussed in an earlier lesson that adjectives and adverbs are sometimes repeated in Jamaican Creole. Some nouns, pronouns, and verbs are also repeated. Adjectives, adverbs, nouns, pronouns, and verbs are not typically repeated in English.

Repetition of Nouns

Nouns that are repeated can be 'repetition dependent.' This means that if the word is used as a single word, it would not make sense.

Here are some examples:

Noun	Meaning
soc-soc	a flavored, frozen drink
reeh-reeh	some identified thing/s
passa-passa	a contentious situation

They can also be repeated for emphasis or to suggest an extreme extent or amount. In this case, they are not repetition dependent. For example:

Noun	Meaning
bag bag	a lot of bags
rubbish rubbish	a lot of rubbish/bits of rubbish
man man	a lot of men

Here are some examples of how these nouns are used:

Jamaican Creole	English
Nof likk'l <u>rubbish rubbish</u> inna di yaad.	A lot of/bits of <u>rubbish</u> are in the yard.
Unnu get nof <u>reeh-reeh</u> frau farin.	You got a lot of <u>things</u> from abroad.
Dem involve inna nof <u>passa-passa</u>.	They are involved in <u>a lot of contentious situations</u>.

Repetition of Verbs

Verbs that are repeated can also be 'repetition dependent.' For example:

Verb	Meaning
palla-palla	to do something [particularly, wash clothes or dishes] hurriedly or incompletely
chaka-chaka	to mess up
laba-laba	to talk a lot (especially gossip)

Verbs are sometimes repeated for emphasis or to communicate that something was done in an extraordinary manner or happened repeatedly. In this case, they are not repetition dependent. E. *up* is frequently added to these verbs. For example:

Verb	Meaning
run run	run around/run repeatedly
kick kick	kick severely/repeatedly
knock knock	knock repeatedly

Here are some examples of how these verbs are used:

Jamaican Creole	English
Di bwuay <u>palla-palla</u> im shoes inna di waata.	The boy <u>hurriedly washed</u> his shoes in the water.
Dem <u>chaka-chaka</u> di room.	They <u>messed up</u> the room.
Di man <u>knock knock-up</u> di duo.	The man <u>knocked [repeatedly]</u> on the door.

Repetition of Pronouns

Pronouns are sometimes repeated for emphasis. These pronouns typically describe quantity or amount. These pronouns are not repetition dependent. For example:

Pronoun	Meaning
nof nof	a lot/plenty
E. one one	a few
plenty plenty	a lot/plenty

Here are some examples of how these pronouns are used:

Jamaican Creole	English
Mi wau <u>nof nof</u>.	I want <u>a lot/plenty</u>.
Mi a pick <u>one one</u>.	lit. I am picking <u>one one</u>.
	(*I am picking a few.*)
Gi dem <u>two two</u> each.	lit. Give them <u>two two</u> each.
	(*Give them two each.*)

The Use of A and Fi

Two prepositions are used in Jamaican Creole to mean *to* in English. They are *a* and *fi*. The English word *to* is also used in Jamaican Creole except in some of the instances below where *a* and *fi* are used.

The Use of A

A is used in Jamaican Creole to show:

1. Direction or destination:

E.g., *Wi a head a Kingston.* (E. *We are heading to Kingston*).

2. The position of someone or something (though E. *to* is more frequently used in this case):

E.g., *Di tyeb'l deh a di back a di room.* (E. *The table is to the back of the room*).

In the previous example, the meaning of *a* is better translated as *toward* in English. It indicates that the table is located somewhere toward the back of the room.

The Use of Fi

Fi is only used to form the infinitive of Jamaican Creole verbs:

E.g., *Dem ha fi goh a St. Ann pau Monday.* (E. *They have to go to St. Ann on Monday*).

The Use of Ku

Ku (E. *look*) is used in Jamaican Creole to draw attention to something or someone:

E.g. 1. *Ku pau datdeh!* (E. *Look at that!*)

E.g. 2. *Ku pan da house deh!* (E. *Look at that house there!*)

The Use of Fi and Fa

Fi and *fa* are both used to mean E. *for.* The word *Fi* is more frequently used than *fa*, however.

E.g., *When yuh a come fi wau visit?* (E. *When are you coming for a visit?*).

When *Fa* is used before *ih* or *it,* an *r* is added at the end of the word.

E.g., *Mi haffi goh look far ih* (E. *I have to go look for it*).

When *fi* is used before *ih* or *it,* the two words are pronounced as if they were one word.

E.g., *Mi haffi goh fiit* (E. *I have to go for it*).

Fi is not used at the end of a sentence. *Fa* is always used in this case.

E.g., *Weh yuh a goh fa?* (E. *What are you going for?*).

Gender

In English, people are referred to by gender, male and female. In Jamaican Creole, the masculine gender is sometimes used to refer to both genders. So, it is not uncommon to hear Jamaicans refer to a female as *iih, im, iihself, fihim,* etc.

In English, an animal or baby is referred to as *it.* In Jamaican Creole, a baby is either referred to by actual gender, or the masculine gender is used irrespective of actual gender (especially in rural parishes). An animal is more frequently referred to as the masculine gender *iih* and *im* (E. *he, his,* etc.), although the feminine gender is sometimes used to refer to a female animal.

Practice Exercise 74

Translate the following sentences to Jamaican Creole. Choose a noun, pronoun, or verb in the sentence and use the technique of repetition. Underline the word that is repeated in the English sentence.

1. The boy threw a lot of clothes on the floor.

   _____

2. A lot of children sit idly in the schoolyard after school.

   _____

3. She told everybody the secret, and everybody is upset.

   _____

4. The baby splashed water all over the floor.

   _____

5. They broke the windows in the old house.

   _____

6. Leta accidentally spilled her drink on the bags.

   _____

7. The workers picked one or two apples at a time.

   _____

8. Jimmy eats different meats for lunch each day.

   _____

9. Rain fell every evening for the past week.

_____

10. Mr. Harold plants many vegetables in the garden in front of his house.

_____

Practice Exercise 75

Form your own Jamaican Creole sentences using the technique of repetition with a noun, pronoun, or verb.

1. _____
2. _____
3. _____
4. _____
5. _____
6. _____
7. _____
8. _____
9. _____
10. _____

Practice Exercise 76

Fill in the blanks with the correct word (*a*, *fi*, or *fa*) to complete the sentences.

1. Im a ᴱrun _____ ᴱprime minista soh im kyah mek di ᴱcountry betta.

2. Mi a ᴱhurry ᴱup _____ goh _____ ᴱtown soh mi kyah ketch di ᴱbank bifuo ih cluoz.

3. Mi noh nuo wa demya ᴱuse _____.

4. _____ uop'mn di [E]box, yuh aggo [E]need wau screw[J]jaiva.

5. Dis a _____ [E]Karen, an disya a _____ [E]Simone.

6. _____ [J]di top [J]a [J]di stairs, [J]shi put [J]wau big, green plant.

7. Ih noh [E]call _____.

8. [E]If yuh [E]look _____ di [E]back a di [E]room, yuh wi si di [E]shoes dem.

9. Wi a wyet pan di tiicha _____ [E]tell wi [E]when _____ staat wi [E]class [E]assignment.

10. A di letta mi [E]come _____.

Practice Exercise 77

Translate the completed sentences from Practice Exercise 76 to English.

1. _____
2. _____
3. _____
4. _____
5. _____
6. _____
7. _____
8. _____
9. _____
10. _____

Practice Exercise 78

Construct your own Jamaican Creole sentences usng the words *a*, *fi*, and *fa*.

1. _____
2. _____
3. _____
4. _____
5. _____
6. _____
7. _____
8. _____
9. _____
10. _____

Practice Exercise 79

Use the following words to form sentences that include repetitive nouns, verbs, and pronouns in Jamaican Creole.

aal *adv., prep.* even; regarding
choo-cho/chuo-cho *n.* chayote
jonjo *n.* mold
mi *pron.* I; me

qwaaril *n., v.* quarrel
wadyeh/wedyeh *n.* the other day
ya *adj., adv., n.* here

1. _____
2. _____
3. _____
4. _____
5. _____
6. _____
7. _____

Reading Comprehensions

Reading Comprehension 1

The Essay Competition

[E]Kenisha did hesitant fi enta wau [E]essay [E]competition weh aar [E]English tiicha encorij aar fi paaticipyet inna. Shi neva [E]sure shi did [E]knowledgeable [E]enough bout di [E]topic, [E]but shi [E]tell aar madda an aar faada bout ih, an dem seh shi fi giit a [E]try. Di [E]topic a did '[E]how fi syev di [E]planet frau [E]pollution.' Afta aar [E]parents dem encorij aar, shi [E]decide fi enta di [E]competition.

[E]Kenisha spen nof dyeh inna di laibri afta [E]school a gyadda infamyeshan. [E]When [E]all di adda [E]student dem [E]gone huom [E]long [E]time, [E]Kenisha wudda jos a [E]walk huom. [E]Sometimes aar madda an aar faada [E]get [E]worried bout aar, an dem [E]call aar fi mek [E]sure seh shi syef. [E]Finally, wid nof [E]hours a wok, [E]Kenisha [E]finish aar fos jraaf. Shi [E]bring ih goh a [E]school soh aar tiicha cudda [E]read ih. Aar tiicha sch di essay [E]good, [E]but shi [E]need fi [E]include [E]some muo [E]details. [E]Kenisha haat did [E]feel [E]heavy bikaah shi [E]already spen soh [E]much [E]time pan ih. [E]Despite di discouragement, [E]Kenisha [F]continue fi wok pan di [E]essay.

Afta wau [E]few muo [E]edits [E]by aar tiicha, [E]Kenisha sen aaf aar [E]essay goh a di [E]essay [E]competition [E]committee. Shi neva did a expek [E]much, soh [E]when shi [E]get wau [E]email seh aar [E]essay inna di [E]semi-final, shi did [E]happy. [E]Two [E]week lyeta, [E]Kenisha [E]get waunadda [E]email seh shi inna di [E]final, an shi, aar [E]parents, an aar tiicha [E]invited [E]to di awaad [E]ceremony fi [E]choose di winna. [E]Kenisha tiicha an [E]parents dem did [E]proud a aar, an shi did [E]proud seh aar haad wok a pyeh aaf.

Di dyeh a di awaad [E]ceremony, shi [E]dress inna wau [E]nice [E]dress an aar [E]parents dem [E]bring aar a di [E]hall weh di [E]event a kip. Aar tiicha [E]meet dem deh. Aar [E]parents dem [E]tell aar seh noh matta wa [E]happen, dem [E]still [E]proud a aar.

Di [E]judge dem [E]announce di [E]top chrii winna. [E]Kenisha huop fi hyer aar nyem [E]call laas. [E]When dem [E]announce di [E]person inna tûrd plyes, [E]Kenisha huol aar bret. Den di [E]judge dem [E]announce [E]Kenisha nyem. [E]Kenisha [E]feel [E]sad [E]at fos, [E]but aar tiicha, aar [E]parents dem, an di adda [E]people dem inna di [E]audience [E]cheer aar aan. Iiv'n duo shi neva [E]win, [E]Kenisha did [E]happy fi [E]come seken.

1. What was the topic of the essay?

   _____

2. Who first encouraged Kenisha to enter the essay competition?

   _____

3. How did Kenisha feel about the competition at first?

   _____

4. Where did Kenisha find information about her topic?

   _____

5. Who helped Kenisha to edit her essay?

   _____

6. Where was the award ceremony held?

   _____

7. What did Kenisha wear to the award ceremony?

   _____

8. Who accompanied her to the award ceremony?

   _____

9. How did Kenisha place in the competition?

   _____

10. How did Kenisha feel about her placement in the competition?

   _____

Reading Comprehension 2

Holiday with Grandma Rita and Grandpa Joe

ᴱEvery samma, ᴱShanique an aar bredda dem goh spen ᴱtime a ᴱMorant ᴱBay wid dem Granny ᴱRita an Granpaa ᴱJoe. ᴱMorant ᴱBay deh pan di ᴱeastern ᴱside a di ᴱisland an ᴱShanique, aar ᴱtwo bredda dem, an aar madda haffi tek chrii ᴱbus an wau ᴱtaxi fi ᴱreach deh. Dem madda wudda lef dem deh an goh ᴱback huom a ᴱManchester.

ᴱShanique fyevrit ting fi duh a ᴱMorant ᴱBay a goh a di ᴱseaside. Shi ᴱlove di soun a di wyev dem ᴱwhen dem ᴱcrash oova di ᴱshore. Shi ᴱalso ᴱlove fi si di fishaman dem a jaah dem buot dem ᴱcome a ᴱshore an tek ᴱout di ᴱfish dem. Dem ᴱsell di ᴱfish ᴱto ᴱpeople ᴱwho ᴱcome fi ᴱbuy ᴱevery maanin. Aar ᴱgranny wudda ᴱbuy ᴱfew ᴱfish frau dem, an dem wudda ᴱeat dem di nex dyeh. ᴱWhen dem tan a di ᴱseaside ᴱtill di ᴱsun staat fi ᴱset, di ᴱorange ᴱsplash a di ᴱsun ᴱacross di ᴱsky did ᴱmagnificent.

Pan di wyeh ᴱback frau di ᴱshore, dem wudda tap fi ᴱget ᴱcashew ᴱfruit frau di ᴱtree dem weh ᴱline di ᴱshore. ᴱWhen dem ᴱget huom, dem wudda ketch wau faiya ᴱout a duo an ᴱput dem ᴱcashew ᴱfruit pan ih. Di sumell a ruos ᴱcashew ᴱfill di iivlin ᴱair. ᴱShanique an aar bredda dem wudda den ᴱcrack di ᴱcashew ᴱfruit uopin an tek ᴱout di ᴱnut. Dem ᴱput wau likk'l ᴱsalt pan dem an ᴱeat dem ᴱhot. ᴱGranny seh dat a wau haaty likk'l snack fi 'ketch ᴱup di stomock'.

Inna di maanin, ih did ᴱcommon fi ᴱShanique dem si ᴱsome likk'l groun lizad a ᴱrun bout di back yaad. Dem ha wau ᴱreddish-brown cola. Aar ᴱgranny seh dem kyaah ᴱclimb ᴱtree ᴱnor ᴱwall, an dem jos ᴱrun bout di groun inna di back yaad. A nof ᴱtime ᴱShanique ᴱtry fi goh cluos fi ᴱlook pan ᴱone a dem, ᴱbut dem ᴱcrawl weh ᴱas ᴱsoon ᴱas shi ᴱnear. Aar ᴱgranny seh dem ᴱshy. A neva ᴱlong bifuo ᴱShanique madda ᴱcome ᴱback fi dem fi goh huom. ᴱShanique ᴱalways sopraiz ᴱhow faas di halidyeh ᴱrun aaf ᴱevery samma.

1. Where does Shanique live?

   _____

2. What time of day does the fishermen usually sell their fish?

   _____

3. Who accompanied Shanique and her brother to her grandparent's home?

   _____

4. Where did Shanique's grandparents live?

   _____

5. What did Shanique's grandmother mean by "wau haaty likk'l snack fi 'ketch ᴱup di stomock'"?

   _____

6. What is Shanique's favorite thing to do in Morant Bay?

   _____

7. What did Shanique and her brothers gather from the sea shore?

   _____

8. Where is Morant Bay located?

   _____

9. What creatures roam around the backyard of her grandmother's house?

   _____

10. What time of day is Shanique more likely to see the creatures?

    _____

Reading Comprehension 3

Lady by the River

Wau uol lyedi did ^Elive ^Eby wau riva ^Eall ^Eby aarself. Shi wyek ^Eup inna di maanin, bwuail aar ^Etea an iht ^Epiece a ^Ebread. Shi ^Eweed di ^Egrass an ^Eplant aar ^Eyam dem. An ^Ewhen di ^Etime ^Ecome fi ^Ereap aar ^Eyam dem, shi ^Edig dem ^Eone ^Eby ^Eone ^Eall ^Eby aarself.

Shi ^Ewash aar cluos dem inna wau uol ^Eenamel byesin ^Ean heng dem pan di ^Eline. An ^Ewhen di ^Esun ^Edone ^Ebeat dong pan dem, an daak ^Eclouds gyadda ^Elike ryen aggo ^Efall, shi ^Epick dem ^Eup frau ^Eoff di ^Eline an ^Ebring dem ^Einside ^Eall ^Eby aarself.

^EWhen iivlin jaah ^Enear, shi gyadda ^Eall di ^Efood weh shi ^Ebring ^Efrom aar grong. Shi ^Ecarefully ^Epeel, ^Ewash, an ^Eput di ^Eyam dem inna di ^Epot. ^EWhen shi ^Edone ^Ecook aar likk'l dinna, shi sidong a di likk'l ^Edining tyeb'l an ^Ehappily iht aar dinna ^Eall ^Eby aarself.

Translate the previous passage to English.

_____

_____

_____

_____

_____

_____

_____

_____

_____

_____

_____

Reading Comprehension 4

Anancy and the Chief

ᴱAnancy ᴱdive dong inna di waata an ᴱswim goh dong a di battam. ᴱAll ᴱof ᴱa sodd'n, wau ᴱspout a waata ᴱpush ᴱAnancy ᴱback ᴱup a di ᴱtop. ᴱAnancy ᴱfly ᴱup inna di iyer an jap heavy pan di riva ᴱbank. Im kin oova pan im ᴱback. ᴱAnancy baal ᴱout.

ᴱAnancy ᴱscratch im ᴱhead auh ᴱlook roun ᴱas im ᴱget ᴱup. Di plyes noh ᴱlook ᴱfamiliar ᴱto ᴱAnancy. Im ᴱwalk roun fi a likk'l ᴱbit a ᴱtry ᴱfigure ᴱout weh im deh. ᴱAnancy bok ᴱup inna wau ᴱman weh ᴱdress inna ᴱunusual cluos. Im ha wau ᴱrod inna im han, an im demaan fi nuo wa ᴱAnancy a duh pan im prapati. ᴱAnancy explyen ᴱto di ᴱman seh im did a tek a likk'l ᴱswim an den im en ᴱup inna di ᴱstrange plyes. Di ᴱman goh tan-op pan di riva ᴱbank fi si ᴱhow ᴱAnancy en ᴱup deh, an im jap inna di waata. Di ᴱman cud'n swim, soh ᴱAnancy ᴱjump inna di waata an syev im. Di ᴱman ᴱvow seh im wi gi ᴱAnancy wateva im wau.

Di ᴱman tek ᴱAnancy huom an giim ᴱfood auh wau plyes fi styeh. ᴱAnancy fain ᴱout seh di ᴱman a di ᴱchief fi di villij. ᴱAnancy ᴱget ᴱreally comfateb'l. Im dimaan di bes ᴱroom inna di ᴱhouse. Im aks fi ᴱmoney, ᴱnew cluos, an di ᴱposition a ᴱassistant ᴱto di ᴱchief. ᴱAll a dis di ᴱchief ᴱput ᴱup wid ᴱuntil ᴱone dyeh, di ᴱchief ᴱget soh taiyad a ᴱAnancy ᴱantics dat im aks im ᴱmagician fi ᴱbanish ᴱAnancy ᴱback weh im ᴱcome ᴱfrom. ᴱAnancy neva nuo seh di ᴱchief did ᴱconsult im ᴱmagician. Im goh a ᴱbed ᴱas ᴱusual an wyek ᴱup di nex maanin inna im uon ᴱbed. ᴱAnancy ᴱlose evriting weh im did ᴱget frau di ᴱchief.

Translate the previous passage to English.

———————————————————————

———————————————————————

———————————————————————

———————————————————————

_____

_____

_____

_____

_____

_____

_____

_____

_____

_____

_____

_____

_____

_____

_____

_____

_____

_____

Frequently Asked Questions

Asking About Time

Ho much a clock?	lit. How much is clock?
	(*What time is it?*)
Wa time?	lit. What time?
	(*What time is it?*)
Wa time wi a lef?	lit. What time we are leaving?
	(*At what time are we leaving?*)
Wa time yuh ha?	lit. What time you have?
	(*What time do you have?*)
Yuh nuo a wa time?	lit. You know it is what time?
	(*Do you know what time it is?*)

Asking How Much Something Costs

A ho much dis/dat kaas?	lit. It is how much this/that costs?
	(*How much does this/that cost?*)
A ho much fi dis/dat?	lit. It is how much for this/that?
	(*How much is it for this/that?*)
Ho much dis/dat kaas?	lit. How much this/that costs?
	(*How much does this/that cost?*)
Ho much fi dis/dat?	lit. How much for this/that?
	(*How much is it for this/that?*)
Wa a di kaas a dis/dat?	What is the cost of this/that?

Asking About Location of Places, Things, or People

Weh di puos office deh?	lit. Where the post office is?
	(*Where is the post office?*)
Weh mi kyah fain wau cambio?	lit. Where I can find a cambio?
	(*Where can I find a cambio?*)
Weh yuh deh?	lit. Where you are?
	(*Where are you?*)
Weh yuh from?	lit. Where you from?
	(*Where are you from?*)
Yuh kyah tell mi how fi reach…?	lit. You can tell me how to reach…?
	(*Can you tell me how to get to…?*)

General Questions

A wa?	lit. It is what?
	(*What is it?/What's the matter?*)
Noh true?	lit. No true?
	(*Isn't that true/ Isn't that so?*)
Waa gwaan?	lit. What's going on?
	(*What's up?/What's going on?*)
Wa/weh yuh a duh?	lit. What you are doing?
	(*What are you doing?*)
Wa/weh yuh deh pan?	lit. What you are on?
	(*What are you up to/What are you doing?*)
Weh yuh nyem?	lit. What you name?
	(*What is your name?/What are you named?*)
Who dat/datdeh?	lit. Who that?
	(*Who is that?*)

Commonly Used Expressions

A good.	lit. It is good (usually used with irony to mean: *serves you right*).
A soh dem tan.	lit. It is how they stay. *(That is how they are (characteristically)).*
A soh di ting set up.	lit. It is how the thing is set up. *(That's how life is.)*
Come ya, man.	Come here, man.
Cool noh, man.	lit. Cool no, man. *(Chill out, man.)*
Evriting kris.	lit. Everything ok. *(Everything is ok.)*
Ku deh.	lit. Look there. *(Look at that.)*
Ku pau yuh.	lit. Look on you. *(Look at you.)*
Ku ya.	lit. Look here. *(Look at this.)*
Kum-out.	Come out (can also mean: *get out*).
Main deh.	lit. Mind there. *(Move away from there/Be careful.)*
Mi come frau…	lit. I come from… *(I am from…)*
Mi dideh.	lit. I am there (can also mean: *I will be there.*)

Mi gone.	lit. I gone.
	(*I'm gone/Goodbye.*)
Mi naah lie yuh.	lit. I am not lying you.
	(*I'm not lying to you.*)
Mi nyem…	lit. My name…
	(*My name is…*)
Mi saat out.	lit. I sort out.
	(*I am doing good/doing ok.*)
Mi wi link yuh.	lit. I will link you.
	(*I will link up with you [at a later date/time].*)
No problem, man.	(Although not Jamaican Creole, it is very commonly used in Jamaica.)
Put ih up.	lit. Put it up.
	(*Put it away for the future.*)
Right ya now.	lit. Right here now.
	(*Right now/At this moment.*)
Saat ih out/saat out…	lit. Sort it out/Sort out.
	(*Get it done.*)
Yeh, man.	Yes, man.
Yuh done nuo.	lit. You done know.
	(*You know it/You already know.*)
Yuh lucky.	lit. You lucky.
	(*You are lucky.*)
	(Used with irony to mean: *That is your misfortune/You deserve whatever misfortune befell you.*)
Yuh siit?	lit. You see it?
	(*You see what it is I'm saying?*)
Yuh si mi?	lit. You see me?
	(*You see what it is I'm saying?*)
Yuh ziit?	lit. You see it?
	(*You see what it is I'm saying?*)
Yuh zi mi?	lit. You see me?
	(*You see what it is I'm saying?*)

Frequently Used Jamaican Proverbs

The following proverbs are commonly used in Jamaica Creole. As with English proverbs, the syntax of proverbs in Jamaican Creole is not necessarily used in everyday conversation, however, proverbs are frequently thrown in to express complex idea with simple words. Words in parenthesis are inserted for better understanding of the proverb.

Jamaican Proverb	Translation
Anno syem dyeh [E]leaf jap inna waata ih ra'n.	It is not same day [that] leaf drops in water it [will] rot.
[E]Bad [E]luck wos dau obya.	Bad luck [is] worse than obeah.
	(*Obeah is a belief system that involves rituals and curses, much like witchcraft and voodoo.*)
Chicken merry, hawk deh [J]near.	Chicken [is] merry, [but] hawk is near.
[E]Cockroach noh bizniz inna [E]fowl [E]fight.	Cockroach [has] no business in fowl fight.
Cowad [E]man kip soun buon.	[a] Coward man keeps sound bones.
Doppi nuo [E]who fi frai'n.	[a] Ghost knows who to frighten.
[E]Every mikk'l mek a mokk'l.	Every bit makes a lot.
Fos [E]laugh anno [E]laugh.	First laugh is not laugh.
	(*Its always best to have the last laugh.*)

Jamaican Proverb	Translation
[E]Fowl weh [E]feed a yaad [E]easy fi ketch.	Fowl that feeds at [a] home is easy to catch.
[E]Hag seh di fos waata yuh si, yuh [E]wash.	Hog says the first water you see, you wash.
[E]Hungry mek puss nyam paach caan.	Hunger makes puss eat parched corn.
[E]If [E]fish weh goh a riva battam [E]tell yuh seh shaak dong deh, [E]believe ih.	If fish that goes to river bottom tells you that shark is down there, believe it.
[E]If yuh wau [E]good, yuh nuoz haffi [E]run.	If you want good, your nose has to run.
	(*If you want to achieve, you have to work hard.*)
Mi chuo mi caan; mi noh [E]call noh [E]fowl.	I threw my corn; I didn't call any fowls.
Noh chob'l chob'l [E]till chob'l chob'l yuh.	Don't trouble trouble until trouble troubles you.
One, one [J]cuoco, full [J]baaskit.	One, one cocoa, full basket.
	(*Each cocoa helps to fill a basket.*)
[E]Puss auh daag noh ha di syem [E]luck.	Puss and dog do not have the same luck.
Wa noh [E]dead, noh dashweh.	What is not dead, don't throw away.
Wa noh [E]kill, fah'n; wa noh fah'n figah'n.	What doesn't kill, fattens; what doesn't fatten [is] forgotten.
Weh ih maaga, a deh ih pap.	Where it is slim, it is there it breaks.
[E]Who kyaah hyeh aggo [E]feel; finga mash, noh badda [E]cry.	Who cannot hear will feel; finger mashed, don't bother [to] cry.
	(*If you refuse to listen to reason, you will suffer the consequences.*)

About the Author

The author was born and grew up in the hills of Clarendon in Jamaica. She is also the author of *Jamaican Creole Tenses* and *Speak Jamaican: A Guide To Fluency.* She works in the field of psychology, but writing has remained one of her greatest passions. The author has the desire to see Jamaican Creole legitimized as a language. She hopes that this book will aid in that process.

www.ingramcontent.com/pod-product-compliance
Lightning Source LLC
Chambersburg PA
CBHW060523130626
46553CB00002B/624